HEALING THE WOUNDS OF REJECTION

HEALING THE WOUNDS OF REJECTION

Moving Forward with Strength,
Confidence, and the Ability to Trust Again

JOYCE MEYER
& GINGER STACHE

NEW YORK • NASHVILLE

Copyright © 2025 by Joyce Meyer and Ginger Stache

Cover design by Catherine Reifschneider. Cover copyright © 2025 by Hachette Book Group, Inc.

Hachette Book Group supports the right to free expression and the value of copyright. The purpose of copyright is to encourage writers and artists to produce the creative works that enrich our culture.

The scanning, uploading, and distribution of this book without permission is a theft of the author's intellectual property. If you would like permission to use material from the book (other than for review purposes), please contact permissions@hbgusa.com. Thank you for your support of the author's rights.

FaithWords
Hachette Book Group
1290 Avenue of the Americas, New York, NY 10104
faithwords.com
@FaithWords / @FaithWordsBooks

First Edition: September 2025

FaithWords is a division of Hachette Book Group, Inc. The FaithWords name and logo are registered trademarks of Hachette Book Group, Inc.

The publisher is not responsible for websites (or their content) that are not owned by the publisher.

The Hachette Speakers Bureau provides a wide range of authors for speaking events. To find out more, go to hachettespeakersbureau.com or email HachetteSpeakers@hbgusa.com.

FaithWords books may be purchased in bulk for business, educational, or promotional use. For information, please contact your local bookseller or the Hachette Book Group Special Markets Department at special.markets@hbgusa.com.

Print book interior design by Kristen Andrews

Library of Congress Cataloging-in-Publication Data has been applied for.

ISBNs: 978-1-5460-0929-0 (hardcover), 978-1-5460-0957-3 (large type), 978-1-5460-0931-3 (ebook)

Printed in the United States of America

LSC-H

Printing 1, 2025

CONTENTS

Introduction	vii
Part 1: Tossed Aside	1
Chapter 1: Created for Acceptance (Joyce and Ginger)	3
Chapter 2: My Story (Joyce)	15
Chapter 3: My Story (Ginger)	25
Chapter 4: An Epidemic of Rejection (Ginger)	33
Chapter 5: Hope on the Horizon (Joyce)	43
Part 2: The Lies of Rejection	55
Chapter 6: Shaped by Rejection (Ginger)	57
Chapter 7: Rooted in Rejection (Joyce)	71
Chapter 8: The Lens of Rejection (Ginger)	83
Chapter 9: Walls of Protection (Joyce)	95
Chapter 10: Perfection and Rejection (Joyce)	105
Part 3: The Pathway to Healing	117
Chapter 11: Reject the Lies of Rejection (Ginger)	119
Chapter 12: Accepting Yourself (Joyce)	133
Chapter 13: Your Past Is Not Your Future (Ginger)	145
Chapter 14: Hurting People Hurt People (Joyce)	155

Part 4: Goodbye, Insecurity; Hello, Peace   165

Chapter 15: Nurturing Confidence (Ginger)   167
Chapter 16: Developing Healthy Relationships (Joyce)   179
Chapter 17: Five Choices That Bring Hope and
               Healing (Ginger)   193

Conclusion   207
Appendix: Fighting for the Rejected   211
Source Notes   215

INTRODUCTION

Joyce

The world is full of people who feel invisible, dismissed, or rejected to the core. More and more people find themselves betrayed and disposed of by spouses, misused by people meant to protect them, canceled by the crowd, or experiencing countless other painful dismissals. Perhaps you are one of them, and you know firsthand that rejection is a powerful force.

I have a particularly heavy burden right now to fight back against the damage rejection is wreaking in people's lives. God has put an urgency in my heart to help people heal from the pain, isolation, and devastation of rejection. This is an extraordinarily timely subject, and I believe God has many important lessons to teach us about how to find freedom from rejection and emerge from it stronger, more confident, and able to trust again.

Rejection is painful and can cause severe long-term damage in the soul (mind, will, and emotions). But thankfully, Jesus is our Healer and can heal us anywhere we hurt. God's Word tells us that He heals our wounds and broken hearts (Psalm 147:3). Even though people in our lives may reject us, God accepts us and loves us unconditionally. He accepts us the way we are, and helps us become the best we can be.

I think more people may be facing rejection today than ever before. The world is filled with angry people who are insensitive to the ways they may affect others. Children are often neglected because their parents are too busy and are dealing with problems of their own. At the same time, some young people have decided to have no contact with their parents. They simply act as though they don't even know their parents for a variety of reasons. Often, these reasons are based on differences of opinion. But even when opinions are strong, it is sad—even tragic—to see families fall apart. Today, people speak of being tolerant, yet they will cut off relationships with the people who raised them. In years past, I can remember a lot of families that held and expressed strong opinions, and sometimes voices were raised in family settings, but when all was said and done, people valued family enough to remain in relationship. They didn't simply walk away from one another.

In addition, the divorce rate is high; divorces of people age fifty and over have increased. Many men involved in these marriages have left their spouses for younger women, which usually makes the wives feel tossed aside and unlovable. Domestic abuse is at an all-time high: The Rape, Abuse & Incest National Network reports that "one in 9 girls and 1 in 20 boys under the age of 18 experience sexual abuse or assault."[1] Young people may also deal with cyberbullying, something unheard of until recent years. Peer pressure is overwhelming for young people. Not only that, according to the National Conference of State Legislatures, "Each year, an estimated 4.2 million youth and young adults experience homelessness in the United States, 700,000 of which are unaccompanied minors."[2] Another 443,000 children are in foster care. The most frequent form of child abuse is simply neglect, which is just another way of saying "You are unimportant, and you are not worth my time." All of these situations are absorbed as profound rejection.

When we consider these statistics, it is easy to see why rejection seems to be an epidemic. It touches all of us, so the question is: What is the antidote? Unless we can firmly take hold of a deep security in who we are, feelings of rejection—and therefore

Introduction

worthlessness—will continue to plague us. However, knowing how much God loves and accepts us—and how valuable we are—will give us the confidence to be like the apostle Paul, who wasn't bothered by what people thought of him because he knew that only God could be his judge (1 Corinthians 4:3–4).

The fear of rejection can lead to people-pleasing, and constantly trying to please others is a miserable way to live. If people are rooted in rejection, that root has many little offshoots that affect their lives and especially their behavior in relationships.

If people are secure and confident, rejection may not affect them much. However, for someone who is insecure and looking for acceptance and approval, being rejected leads to stronger feelings of worthlessness and makes them feel more flawed than they did previously. My husband, Dave, is so secure that I doubt he would even know if someone were rejecting him—and if he did, he wouldn't care. On the other hand, I come from a background of sexual abuse, abandonment, criticism, and divorce due to infidelity, so I have experienced a great deal of rejection that left me insecure, in addition to posing other challenges in my soul. Because of this, I believe I can help other people who are suffering from the wounds of rejection to be healed and made whole.

Healing from rejection isn't easy by any means, but God has healed me, and He will heal you also if you are willing to work with Him.

I'm very happy to be collaborating with Ginger Stache on this book. I invited her to write with me for several reasons. Ginger brings her own unique experiences with rejection, and together, I believe we can help even more people. She shares my urgency to see others overcome the wounds of rejection, and she has a beautiful heart for God and for people. She has worked with Joyce Meyer Ministries for more than twenty years, currently as chief creative officer, and she regularly appears with me on my television program, *Enjoying Everyday Life*. Ginger is an excellent writer and storyteller who draws people in. She is a good friend, and I know you will love her as I do.

Not everyone feels rejected for the same reasons, but it all hurts. There is power in sharing our stories—power that can help to defeat the enemy's plan to use rejection to derail God's good plan for us. In this book, you will read stories of people who have dealt with severe rejection for different reasons, and you may see yourself in these pages. I know the stories you will read in this book—including mine and Ginger's—will help and encourage you. And we will teach you how to handle rejection differently from how you may have handled it before.

I find it interesting that no person has ever been as rejected as Jesus was, but there is no biblical evidence that these experiences distracted Him. They may have hurt Him, but not enough to take His attention away from what His Father sent Him to earth to do. He certainly didn't allow His feelings to control Him. He understood human nature and did not entrust Himself to the people around Him (John 2:24–25 AMP). This means He didn't put more confidence in people than would have been wise. He knew who He was, where He came from, and what He was here to do—and that did not change based on people's acceptance or rejection of Him.

I have discovered in my life that each time God was ready to promote me to the next level of ministry, I was also hit with major rejection from people I loved and trusted. I think rejection is one of the devil's favorite tools, and he uses it to torment people and hinder them from fulfilling their destiny. But he does not need to succeed.

In this book, Ginger and I desire to help you receive healing for the wounds of rejection and grow to a place where you can deal with rejection in a healthy way and be secure enough to know

Introduction

that God loves and accepts you completely. If you put your trust in Him, He will always take care of you and give you people who love and accept you. You can be confident and secure and not let what other people do or say affect you in negative ways.

To help you apply the lessons this book teaches, we've included a section titled "Lean in Closer" at the end of each chapter. These questions are designed to prompt you to think about your life and lean into God and His Word in ways that will help you process your experiences with rejection and move toward strength, confidence, and wholeness.

It's time for you to enjoy freedom and healing.

PART 1

Tossed Aside

He was despised and rejected by mankind, a man of suffering, and familiar with pain. Like one from whom people hide their faces he was despised, and we held him in low esteem.

Isaiah 53:3

CHAPTER 1

Created for Acceptance

Joyce and Ginger

By faith we have been made acceptable to God. And now, thanks to our Lord Jesus Christ, we have peace with God.
                                    Romans 5:1 CEV

Rejection hurts, and one reason it is so painful is that we are created by God to be loved and accepted. The Bible says that God created us in His own image (Genesis 1:27), and He designed us for love (John 3:16), belonging (1 Corinthians 3:23), and His glory (Isaiah 43:7). He also designed us for companionship (Genesis 2:18). We were created for acceptance. So, when we are rejected, it violates an inherent need that is built into our hearts—a part of who we are.

Reading some of the definitions of the word *reject* reveals the deep-rooted pain it carries: "to refuse to accept,"[3] "to cast out or off,"[4] "to throw out as useless."[5] Let's keep it simple; in the children's version of their dictionary, Merriam-Webster defines *reject* like this: "to throw away as useless or unsatisfactory."[6] These words alone can do more damage than most physical blows. These wounds cut deep.

Traumatic rejection goes far beyond hurt feelings. We may not even realize how rejection has shaped us and still influences us. It's insidious. It digs in its roots and its poison spreads throughout our system. But truth can set us free (John 8:32).

> *You may not realize how rejection shapes you.*

When we have received Christ as our Lord and Savior, we are God's children (John 1:12; Galatians 3:26). Because we are His children, He loves and accepts us and will never reject us, but we don't have this same guarantee from people. God does, however, give us the tools we need to stand on our *true* value rather than on the acceptance of others. He also gives us everything we need to deal with the real hurt that comes when they do reject us.

Do you ever feel that everyone needs you, but no one really

wants you? Rejection comes in many forms. A friend betrays you. A spouse is unfaithful or walks away. You're passed over for the promotion you worked hard for. A child refuses your

> *Do you feel that others need you, but no one wants you?*

love. You're mistreated because of your gender, skin color, or ethnicity. A parent doesn't protect you as they should. You may even be rejected for Christ's sake, simply because you are a Christian. The list of ways and reasons you can be rejected is seemingly endless, and the hurt can be excruciating.

Rejection is not a matter of *if*; it's a matter of *when*. We all face rejection. You are not alone in this struggle. With

> *Everyone faces rejection.*

God's help, you can learn to respond differently and to decide how much power you will allow rejection to have over your life. You may even discover that God can use it for your good.

Jesus Himself lived the pain of rejection. In Him, we have a safe haven, a high priest who understands and has sympathy for us (Hebrews 4:15). He faced rejection at nearly every turn. Jesus even knew what it was like to feel unwelcome and unloved by those who should have known Him best, the people of His own home, the town of Nazareth. Matthew 13:57–58 says the people there didn't accept Him; He was considered "without honor." This passage goes on to say their rejection had consequences and that Jesus did not do many miracles there because of their lack of faith.

Jesus had a mission, and He knew that the very people He came to earth to help, along with the religious leaders of His day, were intent on killing Him. His brothers wanted Him to perform miracles to prove who He was because even they did not believe in Him (John 7:4–5). Peter, one of Jesus' closest disciples, denied Him when he was being questioned prior to His crucifixion (Luke 22:54–62), and another disciple, named Judas, literally sold him out (Matthew

26:14–16). Can you imagine how that must have felt? He loved His disciples and had just washed their feet (John 13:2–5), a gesture of devotion and humility, yet they turned their backs on Him. You can be sure He understands how you feel when you are rejected.

When Jesus sent His disciples out two by two to preach the gospel, heal the sick, and do other miracles, He told them that if they went to any town that rejected them, they should shake the dust of it off their feet and move on to the next (Matthew 10:14). He was saying, basically, "Don't let their rejection stop you from reaching your goal."

There is also great comfort in this:

> He who hears and heeds you [disciples] hears and heeds Me; and he who slights and rejects you slights and rejects Me; and he who slights and rejects Me slights and rejects Him who sent Me.
>
> Luke 10:16 AMPC

Here, Jesus is saying, essentially, "Don't take it personally, because the One they are actually rejecting is our Heavenly Father, the One who sent Me."

Scripture includes many other references to times when Jesus faced rejection, such as:

> He was despised and rejected by mankind, a man of suffering, and familiar with pain. Like one from whom people hide their faces he was despised, and we held him in low esteem.
>
> Isaiah 53:3

> He was in the world, and the world was made through him, yet the world did not know him. He came to his own, and his own people did not receive him.
>
> John 1:10–11 ESV

> If the world hates you, know that it has hated me before it hated you.
>
> John 15:18 ESV

> The stone the builders rejected has become the cornerstone.
>
> Psalm 118:22

Without question, Jesus knows intimately the pain of rejection. God doesn't tell us to "just get over it." His heart breaks with ours. He collects our tears and binds up our wounds (Psalm 56:8 NLT; 147:3). He is our healer.

There Is One Who Never Rejects You

You truly are created for acceptance. You are chosen by God, and you are His friend. You are so very special to Him. He will *never* reject you. The verses below assure you of this:

> *You are chosen by God.*

> I no longer call you servants, because a servant does not know his master's business. Instead, I have called you friends, for everything that I learned from my Father I have made known to you. You did not choose me, but I chose you and appointed you so that you might go and bear fruit—fruit that will last—and so that whatever you ask in my name the Father will give you.
>
> John 15:15–16

> Even as [in His love] He chose us [actually picked us out for Himself as His own] in Christ before the foundation of the world, that we should be holy (consecrated and

set apart for Him) and blameless in His sight, even above reproach, before Him in love.

Ephesians 1:4 AMPC

For we know, brothers and sisters loved by God, that he has chosen you.

1 Thessalonians 1:4

Take time every morning to think about how much God loves and accepts you. Even just a little time spent this way can make a big difference. He loves us, but we must receive His love to personally experience it. God doesn't love us because we deserve it, but because He wants to. God is love, and everything He does in our lives is done out of love, even if we don't understand how He's moving. He doesn't cause people to hurt us, but if they do and we trust Him, then He will work it out for good (Romans 8:28).

Because we are created to be loved, valued, and accepted, when we are rejected, it hurts. But we can choose not to let it destroy us. When you feel rejected by someone, remember that you are special and chosen by God and that He considers you to be His friend. This is much better than being surrounded by superficial friends. He is a friend who sticks closer than a brother (Proverbs 18:24).

You Are a Delight

Not only does God love you and consider you a friend, but He also delights in you. This is such a beautiful revelation. We like to say that you make God smile. We might even say you bring a twinkle to His eye. If *to reject* means "to throw away as useless or unsatisfactory," as defined previously, the opposite word may be *to delight*. Merriam-Webster defines *delight* as "a high degree of gratification or pleasure: joy" and "extreme satisfaction."[7] The Bible says that God delights in you.

> God delights in you.

> The Lord your God is with you, the Mighty Warrior who saves. He will take great delight in you; in his love he will no longer rebuke you, but will rejoice over you with singing.
>
> Zephaniah 3:17

> He brought me out into a spacious place; he rescued me because he delighted in me.
>
> Psalm 18:19

And Micah 7:18 tells us He "delights in steadfast love" (ESV). His exuberant love for you is resolute.

It is also true that when we delight in the Lord—when we enjoy who He is, relax in His loving care, and relish spending time with Him—He promises to give us the desires of our hearts (Psalm 37:4). This isn't about our frivolous desires; this is His meeting the deepest needs of our soul, including the healing our hearts yearn for.

It is comforting to know that God loves us, but sometimes we need a touch from people. God works through people, and I (Joyce) have learned to take every compliment I receive—every favor, every gift, and every kindness—as though it comes from God.

Recently, Dave tripped over the carpet and fell into a glass coffee table. The glass didn't break, and he wasn't hurt at all. He didn't say, "Boy, am I lucky that I didn't get hurt." He said, "God's angels were all around me protecting me." Let's give God credit for what He does instead of calling His work "luck" or "coincidence." Watch for Him, because He is working in your life.

We also want to encourage you to expect good things to happen in your life. Try to be conscious and aware of God's love (1 John

4:16). Watch for all the seemingly little things He does in your life, and it will encourage you—an answered prayer, a little favor, finding a parking space right in front of a store when the parking lot is full and it's pouring down rain. Are these coincidences? We don't think so. We think these are winks from God letting you know He is watching over you.

Don't Be Separated from God's Love

Rejection touches our lives and leaves its mark in many ways. When a person's spouse leaves, the one left behind is being rejected, and it hurts. When children grow up without the love of a parent, they are hurt, and this often affects their personality and relationships in a negative way. They may be insecure, lack confidence, feel angry without knowing why, or become people-pleasers in an effort to be loved instead of rejected. Some rejection may be misperceived, imagined, or rooted in self-protection—a result of the wounds of previous rejections. In this book, we will try to cover these issues and more, and we will give you the tools you need to avoid falling into the trap the devil has set for you: the trap of rejection.

> *Avoid falling into the trap of rejection.*

Together, we will discover a pathway that leads from heartbreak to courage, from betrayal to overcoming, from painful secrets to freedom, and from insecurity to acceptance and courage.

Right here and now, let us begin with this important determination: We will not allow rejection to separate us from our true source of acceptance and love. The first thing to do in every rejection or disappointment with people is to remember how much God loves you and to refuse to let anything separate you from His love. Turn to God and ask Him to comfort you. He is the Comforter and can soothe you in ways no one else can (2 Corinthians 1:3–4).

Read carefully these words from Romans 8:35–39:

> Who shall separate us from the love of Christ? Shall trouble or hardship or persecution or famine or nakedness or danger or sword? As it is written: "For your sake we face death all day long; we are considered as sheep to be slaughtered." No, in all these things we are more than conquerors through him who loved us. For I am convinced that neither death nor life, neither angels nor demons, neither the present nor the future, nor any powers, neither height nor depth, nor anything else in all creation, will be able to separate us from the love of God that is in Christ Jesus our Lord.

Consider reading this passage a few times, and let its truth soak into your soul. Let it remind you not to allow the hurt you presently feel to separate you from the knowledge that God loves you in Christ Jesus.

As you read this book, take your time and think about the things we share. So often in life, we are in such a hurry to get finished that we miss what the journey was all about. Take time to meditate on the truth that you are accepted by God.

God tells the Old Testament prophet Jeremiah:

> Before I formed you in the womb I knew [and] approved of you [as My chosen instrument], and before you were born I separated and set you apart, consecrating you; [and] I appointed you as a prophet to the nations.
>
> Jeremiah 1:5 AMPC

Jeremiah was predestined for a good work, but he could have turned away from it. God told him what His will was, and though

Jeremiah was insecure and felt he was too young (Jeremiah 1:6), he stepped out in faith to fulfill God's word.

The same is true for us. God has predestined and prearranged a good life for us so that we might walk in it. This usually requires stepping out in faith. Ephesians 2:10 (AMPC) says:

> For we are God's [own] handiwork (His workmanship), recreated in Christ Jesus, [born anew] that we may do those good works which God predestined (planned beforehand) for us [taking paths which He prepared ahead of time], that we should walk in them [living the good life which He prearranged and made ready for us to live].

Keep Your Eyes on Jesus

Even though you may be experiencing rejection in some area of your life right now, God is also doing a lot of good in your life. Keep your eyes on the good things instead of ruminating on the rejection. Confess aloud the good things the Bible says about you—positive, Scripture-based statements such as:

- "I am accepted by God" (see John 6:37).
- "God loves me unconditionally" (see Romans 5:8).
- "I don't have to be afraid because God is always with me" (see Isaiah 41:10).
- "God is currently working in my life and healing all my wounds" (see Psalm 147:3).
- "God gives me favor with the right people" (see Psalm 5:12).

Repeating these truths will increase your faith, and because God's Word has healing power in it, it will aid in your healing. Perhaps you've felt unwanted, overlooked, or recklessly tossed aside. Maybe you've been brutally betrayed or lost a relationship that meant a lot to you. We are so very sorry. We know it hurts. This journey of healing is a hard one. It takes time and determination. But the fight is worth it. The Word of God is medicine for our wounded souls. It is what God uses to teach us truth and heal us, and He will use it in your life, too. His Word gives you hope when you feel hopeless.

Lean in Closer

1. Thoughtfully consider why you picked up this book. Fearlessly and honestly reflect on the ways you have experienced rejection.

2. What does it mean to you to know you were made by God for acceptance? How does it lighten any shame or guilt you may have felt about the pain of rejection?

3. Respond to the question "Do you ever feel like everyone needs you, but no one really wants you?" What impact does this question have on you?

4. What does it mean to you that Jesus experienced rejection, just as you have experienced it? With that in mind, why are these verses important to you?
    - Isaiah 53:3

- Matthew 13:57–58

  _____
  _____

- John 7:4–5

  _____
  _____

- John 1:10–11 ESV

  _____
  _____

5. How does the way you see yourself change when you realize that God has chosen you, that He calls you His friend, and that He delights in you?

   _____
   _____

6. Rejection tries to separate you from the love of God. Write down a few ways you will keep the truth of God's amazing love in the forefront of your thoughts.

   _____
   _____

CHAPTER 2

My Story

Joyce

When my father and my mother forsake me, then the Lord will take care of me.

Psalm 27:10 NKJV

Even though God created us for acceptance, we all experience rejection as we go through life with other people. Rejection does the most damage to our souls when it comes from people we love, trust, and expect to love and care for us. When we don't care about a person or need them in some way, being rejected by them doesn't affect us as deeply. But when a person holds an important place in our lives and they reject and mistreat us, the pain is intense.

Rejection takes many forms. It's much more than simply encountering someone who doesn't like you or doesn't want you around. These are just some of the ways rejection can manifest in a person's life:

- abuse of any kind, including emotional, verbal, physical, and sexual
- abandonment
- not having basic or legitimate needs met
- being ignored or overlooked
- being devalued or disrespected
- being excluded or left out
- being betrayed
- not being listened to or taken seriously
- not being protected
- being the target of someone's anger or rage
- being laughed at, mocked, or ridiculed
- being judged, criticized, or falsely accused

I have experienced everything on the list above, and perhaps you have, too. Some experiences with rejection are minor, and others are major—meaning that some don't seem to affect us much, while others are life-altering rejections that require a lot of healing, perhaps over a long period of time. I remember a particular experience that seems minor compared with other things that happened to me, but it made a huge impact on my soul.

One year, when I was in elementary school, my classmates and I dressed up for Halloween. Most of the girls in my class dressed up as fairies, princesses, or something else considered beautiful. My father never wanted to spend money on things like Halloween costumes, so my mother bought me a cheap, ugly rubber wolf mask. I still remember the pain I felt when I saw how pretty the other girls looked in their costumes and endured their making fun of me, "the ugly wolf." I can even remember hiding in the corner of the schoolyard, hoping they wouldn't see me. That hurt, and I still remember the pain today.

I have also experienced rejection in major ways, and I want to spend the rest of this chapter sharing five situations that affected me significantly. If you can relate in any way to anything I have been through, I hope and pray that as you read my story, you will be filled with hope that God can heal you, restore you, and set you free to live a wonderful life, just as He has done for me.

Sexual Abuse

The first person who rejected me was my father. Interestingly, his rejection of me didn't involve pushing me out of his life, ignoring me, pretending I didn't exist, or trying to avoid having a relationship with me. It was worse. This particular rejection was extremely perverted; he rejected me by luring me into the *wrong type* of relationship. Being overlooked or ignored would have been better than what actually happened—years of intimidation, control, and, worst of all, sexual abuse.

My father had a problem with lust, and he began molesting me before I was old enough to start school, as best as I can recall. I'm not positive how old I was, because that is all I can remember about my relationship with him. By the time I was in early elementary school, he was showing me pornography and was grooming me to be a sex partner. As I got older, the abuse intensified until he was having regular intercourse with me. The abuse continued until I was eighteen years old and left home.

When I try to think about my childhood, I mostly remember being afraid all the time. Afraid my father would do it again. Afraid my mother would find out.

> *When I think about my childhood, I remember always being afraid.*

Her finding out frightened me because my father had threatened me not to tell her. He told me what he was doing was "love," so I didn't understand why it had to be a secret. I knew it wasn't right but didn't quite know what to do about it. I was rejected as a daughter. I never remember getting to be a child. I *never* felt safe.

Unmet Needs

The next big thing that made me feel rejected happened a few years later, when I told my mother what my father was doing to me. When she confronted him, he told her I was lying and she chose to believe him, even though I think she knew I was telling the truth. I had a basic, legitimate need for protection—and my mother completely ignored it, leaving me to suffer greatly.

When I was about fourteen years old, my mother had gone to the grocery store and returned home sooner than expected. She caught my father in bed with me, and I secretly breathed a sigh of relief, assured she would now do something to help me. Instead, she walked out of the house, came back two hours later, and never mentioned it again.

I was devastated!

How could a mother know her husband was having sex with her daughter and do nothing about it? The only excuse she ever gave was about thirty years later when she said to me, "I'm sorry for what I let your father do to you. I just couldn't face the scandal." I don't even have words to express how disappointed I was.

Not long afterward, I asked an aunt and uncle to help me, but they didn't want to get involved. I didn't have friends because I wasn't allowed to participate in activities at school, other than to attend classes. My father controlled me and isolated me from others to a great extent, and I can honestly say that once I realized my mother and my family members weren't going to help me, I finally just gave up thinking I would ever get out of the situation until I was old enough to leave home. At that point, I set myself to survive.

> I set myself to survive.

I could tell you hundreds of horrid details, but I simply want to say that I was rooted in rejection from an early age. And until I was in my early forties, all the fruit of my life was colored by that rejection. I didn't even know that rejection was what I was dealing with. I simply reached a point where I knew I had to get away from it.

I left home when I was eighteen, having gotten a job. I packed my few belongings when my father was at work and moved to an apartment I had rented. I thought I left my problem behind me and didn't realize I took it with me in my soul.

Abandonment and Divorce

At eighteen years old, I married the first young man who showed any interest in me. This relationship was a disaster, and it ushered even more rejection into my life. My first husband was more troubled than I was, just in different ways. He abandoned me repeatedly, twice when we were out of town, which meant I had to take a bus home alone. I doubt I can even count the number of times he simply didn't come home and disappeared for two or three months. Then he eventually would come home and tell me how wrong he was and how much he loved me. I fell for this every time and took him back, because the pattern of abuse and rejection I had already experienced in my parents' home had destroyed my belief that I was worthy of anything better.

He left me while I was pregnant but came back after the baby was born. We were together again only a short time before he left to live with another woman. By then, I'd had all I could take, and I divorced him. The five years I was married to him consisted of one rejection after another.

Rejection in Ministry

The next major rejection I experienced took place years later, when God called me into the ministry. I had married Dave by then and had three children. I was very excited about the call of God to teach His Word and expected others to be excited for me, but that was far from what happened. Dave and I were asked to leave our church. All our friends—except two that I can remember—rejected us, and with a couple of exceptions, our extended family members rejected us as well.

I was told I couldn't teach because I didn't have the education or the right personality and because I was a woman. I didn't foresee that any of this would be a problem, because God had anointed me to teach, and I was simply trying to follow what I believed He wanted me to do. All these experiences with rejection were very, very painful. When I look back at how painful those times were, I know that God must have given me the grace to hang on and not cave in to people's desire for me to do what they wanted—instead of following what I believed to be God's will.

Rejection That Led to Freedom

The fifth major rejection I will mention occurred after I had been in ministry for about ten years. I had spent several years teaching two Bible studies each week with about twenty-five or thirty people in attendance. Then, I was a church staff member for several years; I became an associate pastor, Bible college teacher, and head of the women's ministry. I also held a weekly women's meeting, which approximately four hundred women attended.

I eventually felt that God wanted me to leave my position at the church and start Joyce Meyer Ministries. I had a deep desire to teach in many places—not just one—and I wanted to write books. But my pastor had told me I couldn't. He felt I needed to be committed to his vision if I was going to work at the church—and he was right.

Even though I wanted to leave my job to start my own ministry—and even though Dave also believed I needed to leave—I waited two years before leaving. I simply didn't have the courage to do it sooner, and fear held me back. I believe my disobedience (not leaving when I knew I should) opened a door for the devil to come against me with a major attack of rejection. Several ladies who worked with me in the women's ministry turned against me and accused me of things that were not true. Their rejection hurt me so deeply that it took me three years to get over it. However, God used it to push me out of that job, which led to what we know today as Joyce Meyer Ministries.

Rejection hurts deeply.

After I no longer had the security of the job at the church, I was afraid all the time—afraid we wouldn't have enough money to live on, afraid no one would attend the meetings I was having in and around my home in St. Louis, and afraid people wouldn't like or accept me. I lived in fear, but I came to realize the fear was the fruit of the rejection that was deeply rooted in my soul. I was dealing with all the rejection that took place as I left my job while trying to start a new ministry, and it was very difficult and emotionally painful. But I was also determined not to give up, and God's grace was present to enable me to press through and not quit.

All the abuse and rejection that I experienced impacted my life in major ways and left me with many wounds. I had many emotional and relational problems, but I always blamed them on someone else. When God began to open my eyes to the truth that I had problems, I was shocked.

As I mentioned, after my divorce, I met and married Dave. This was in 1967. He was exactly what I needed. Even so, I tried to blame all my problems on him. I always thought that if he would treat me better, pay more attention to me, or spend all his free time with me, then I would be happy. But the truth was that nothing was going to make me happy until I let God work in my life and heal my wounded soul.

As you can see, I experienced many severe rejections, any of which could have derailed me from my true purpose. But those rejections were not the end of my story. God redeemed my pain and was even able to use it for His glory and to help others. My life could have gone in a completely different direction, but I'm so glad I did not allow rejection to stop God from working in me as He desired. I refused to allow rejection to define me, and God had much better plans. He does for you, too!

Lean in Closer

1. In what ways do you relate to Joyce's story?

   _____

   _____

My Story

2. Joyce's mother did nothing when Joyce needed help most and abandoned her to the abuse. How has feeling abandoned impacted you?

   _____
   _____

3. Joyce says she lived in fear. What, if any role, has fear played in your life?

   _____
   _____

4. Joyce writes that she blamed her problems on Dave but finally learned that "nothing was going to make me happy until I let God work in my life and heal my wounded soul." Why is it true that nothing makes us happy apart from God's work and healing in our lives?

   _____
   _____

5. Not even the devastating rejection Joyce experienced could keep her from eventually experiencing the good plan God had for her. What do these verses say to you about the plan God has for you?
   - Isaiah 14:27

   _____
   _____

   - Isaiah 54:17

   _____
   _____

   - Romans 8:28

   _____
   _____

CHAPTER 3

My Story

Ginger

Even my close friend, someone I trusted, one who shared my bread, has turned against me.

Psalm 41:9

I was not born into a world of rejection, as Joyce was, but it found me. And when it did, it hit me like a sucker punch to the gut. I'll never forget *that* day—the day I came to know rejection on an entirely new level. Maybe I should have seen it coming, but I didn't, and that day changed many aspects of my life. To say I was brokenhearted is a massive understatement. This unexpected blow was like a screaming indictment of everything I was not, evidence of my unworthiness, and a huge "I told you so" from latent insecurities looking for a chance to surface.

Of course, I had experienced rejection before. It finds all of us at one time or another, but prior to this, it hadn't impacted me as severely as it did that day. If someone liked me, great! If they didn't, that was okay, too. God blessed me with a naturally confident personality. The way I saw it, if someone rejected me, that person was missing out on a faithful friend and a lot of fun, if I do say so myself.

You see, I was raised to know who God says I am in His Word—thank you, Mom and Dad—and that truth trumped what other people chose to believe about me, along with their darts of rejection. At least it *did* until the shocking day when I discovered my husband had been hiding an ugly secret for years. In that moment, my perception of reality popped like a balloon, and as the air escaped, so did my illusion of security.

I Thought I Knew Him

Tim and I were college sweethearts. Though opposites in so many ways, we laughed a lot, spent most of our time together, and couldn't imagine a future apart. We were best friends and very much in love. So, after we both graduated, we married and moved out of state to begin our careers—he as an industrial engineer and I in television.

Fast-forward fifteen years, and we had built a happy marriage. We were surrounded by good friends, attended a church we loved, and had been blessed with two beautiful daughters. I thought I knew him and that I knew our life together inside and out. But when his addiction to pornography clawed its way to the surface, it became evident that the relationship I thought we shared was only a façade.

He had become more irritable and easily angered. Clearly, something was bothering him. When I asked, he said it was nothing. Then, that fateful day, I walked to the mailbox and, among the bills and junk mail, found pornography. It was labeled with Tim's name and our home address.

I took it to him, and he denied any knowledge of where it could have come from. We argued, and I stormed away. About twenty minutes later, he came to me with tears streaming down his face and told me everything. He'd been caught up in pornography since he was just a boy. He told me how he hated the hold it had on him and that he had hidden it all his life. He didn't know exactly how that piece of mail made its way to our home, but what he was doing online must have caught up with him somehow. The guilt and shame were eating him alive. He said he couldn't stand it anymore.

His betrayal slammed into me like an eighteen-wheeler, knocking me down and leaving me questioning almost everything I thought I knew to be true. My ability to trust, the future I thought we would share, and, in a surprising turn, my confidence, were all victims—crushed under the weight of that secret. At that moment, I had absolutely no empathy for him. I felt betrayed and angry, shocked and foolish, devastated and rejected. *Deeply rejected.*

> *Rejection can leave you feeling shocked and foolish.*

Few of us are immune to the power of rejection. Even the most secure people desire acceptance, and it hurts deeply when people deceive and betray us. In hindsight, I realize I had never experienced the brutal rejection of someone so close, someone I loved so dearly. This was very different. This rejection came at the hands of the man with whom I shared every aspect of my life, the one who knew me like no other and who had promised to love me above all else. Instead, he had lied to me for years. He chose vacant, soulless images over me and deception over our family and all we shared together.

I spiraled downward for a long time, marinating in the pain and nursing the anger into fury. You see, when your spouse is living with an addiction to pornography, the damage is not isolated to that one person. Others will get knocked down by the waves of destruction as well. When I first discovered the truth, those waves hit like a tsunami. When the first wave of outrage eventually swept through, it left behind seas of roiling emotions, ebbing and flowing with feelings I didn't know how to navigate. I had followed Christ all my life. I was a grounded Christian who loved Jesus with all my heart. Yet here I was struggling to focus on who God says I am while reeling from the rejection of the one I loved most.

> *Focus on who God says you are.*

Questions filled my mind.

- Was *everything* a lie?
- How could I trust him again? How could I trust anyone?
- What do I do now? What about our family?
- How could God let this happen to us?

I was caught in those rough seas, bobbing from rage to sadness then tossed back to new heights of fury. I felt as though I was drowning. Disappointment, grief, shame—the emotions were eating me alive. Tim was my best friend, and that was gone, too.

I'm an intelligent woman; how could I have been so wrong? I'm not sure anyone who hasn't experienced these circumstances can understand the depth of the betrayal. A few people told me it's not that big of a deal, that "all men do it." Clearly these people had no concept of the havoc addiction can wreak on us and on our relationships. Others reacted with such disgust that I felt tainted and rejected because of my husband's behavior. It was mortifying.

Can I ever get past this? I asked myself. *Am I overreacting?* These questions continued to torment me.

I had many decisions to make and a life to somehow rebuild, and I didn't know what it would look like. Jesus says in Matthew 5:28 that if anyone looks at a woman with lust, he has already committed adultery with her in his heart. A secret lifestyle of pornography is one of lies and lust, so let's call it what it is: My husband was unfaithful. He and I had terrible conversations, and I had to ask questions I never imagined I would have to ask him of all people. Details I needed to know but could never unhear. It was a long, winding, ugly road.

Choices

In time, when I began to regain my footing, I realized I only had a couple of choices. This situation wasn't just about my marriage; this was about *me*. I could allow this scorching rejection to wreak havoc in my life, as the enemy meant for it to, to be thrown off course, perhaps even fail my children, and veer from God's call on my life. *Or* I could allow God to help me move forward, to heal me, to reveal what He had ahead for me, and to possibly even make me better through this. I knew the latter

> *Learn how to fight back against rejection.*

path was the right choice for me. And God has come through. He's taught me so many things, including where I find *true* security. I know now how to fight back against rejection. Rejection still hurts when it comes, but it has far less power over me than it once did.

I want this for you, too. If you are walking through the devastation of betrayal, a loved one's addiction, abandonment, or any other soul-crushing rejection experience, I am so sorry. The pain is nearly impossible to describe. God has declared two people in a marriage to be one flesh (Genesis 2:24), so when one is disloyal, it is shocking and feels a bit like one of your own hands slapping you across the face. You are left with the deep wounds of emotional and relational injury. Even after those wounds heal—and yes, they can heal—some scars remain. I know because I bear those scars.

For a while, I thought this betrayal and the rejection I experienced was the end of my world. It wasn't. And it won't be for you, either.

I don't write this because I'm angry. Oh, I was! But I'm not any longer. I write to say you are not alone. I write because so many of us need help and freedom. You shouldn't have to hide in the shadows of rejection or shame and embarrassment. I write to tell you that even in the face of the nightmare you may be going through, you have good days ahead to look forward to.

Now I can say I'm grateful for that fateful day and what I found in the mailbox. I have no doubt that it was God's hand at work revealing the secret. I'm not glad we had to walk through the ugliness, but I am thankful to be free of it. Jesus says in John 8:32 that the truth will set you free. And Jesus said, quoting the Old Testament prophet Isaiah:

> He has sent Me to heal the brokenhearted, to proclaim liberty to the captives and recovery of sight to the blind, to set at liberty those who are oppressed.
>
> Luke 4:18 NKJV

My Story

Jesus came to set us free—free from deception and lies, free from addiction and bondage and rejection of all kinds. I had been blind, and He gave me sight. Discovering what was going on in our home hurt incredibly, but I would rather walk in the light of truth than remain in the darkness of secrets. In the light, there is healing.

> In the light, there is healing.

I share my journey with the prayer that something I learned will help others survive the storm and to offer hope. Many years have passed since the day my world came crashing down, and God has brought restoration and healing to me, to Tim, and to our marriage. Our relationship is stronger now than ever—but it took a great deal of tears, prayer, counseling, and brutal honesty to get there.

This may sound harsh, but I also believe that if things had gone differently, had Tim not fought as hard as he did and had we ended up walking separate paths, I would still be okay. I would still be right here—loving God and aware that He is the One who has never rejected me and never will.

I'm not the same person; that day changed me. I've learned a great deal. I'm stronger and more compassionate, and I know Christ on a deeper level. If you find yourself walking through a similar rejection—or any type of rejection—my prayer for you is that in Joyce's story and mine, and in these pages, you will also find a new beginning, a catalyst moving you toward your healing. People will hurt us; relationships will change and fail. But you don't have to let rejection define you. Your security is not based on your circumstances or the people in your life. God has so much more for you. You, too, will heal and grow and flourish as you allow God to heal you from the rejection you have experienced.

Lean in Closer

1. In what ways do you relate to Ginger's story?
   _____
   _____

2. Think of the betrayal and rejection you may have experienced. Can you connect with the "seas of roiling emotions" that Ginger describes?
   _____
   _____

3. Ginger explains that because of all God has taught her and done in her life, rejection has less power over her now than it did previously. In what ways do you look forward to rejection having less power over you?
   _____
   _____

4. Read Luke 4:18 (NKJV). How can God work through truth, even painful truth, to bring freedom and healing?
   _____
   _____

5. How can you apply the following sentences to your life? "But you don't have to let rejection define you. Your security is not based on your circumstances or the people in your life."
   _____
   _____

CHAPTER 4

An Epidemic of Rejection

Ginger

In this world you will have trouble. But take heart! I have overcome the world.

John 16:33

The story of heartache and rejection, this journey of dismissal and embarrassment, is not just Joyce's story or mine. It's the story of far too many. Your path may be different from ours. It may not have been set in motion by a painful secret; it may have happened in some other painful way. But in the coming pages, we all will find parts of ourselves. There are many roads that lead to a broken heart, and thankfully, God has also provided a pathway out of each one. The journey out of rejection and into wholeness is not for the faint-hearted. It's hard. And you'll have to fight. You'll take steps forward and a step back now and then. But don't give up! The Lord carries healing for all. *No one* is excluded.

You may have experienced rejection early in life. Perhaps you were unwanted or neglected by the very people who were meant to love and care for you. You may have come up against so many bullies and been so ostracized through the years that those scratches, scrapes, and bruises inflicted by different people eventually festered, the infection drilled deep, and new wounds piled on top of old ones until you didn't think you could handle even one more. Or you may have endured the shock of learning that someone you trusted did what you never imagined would happen. Maybe it was a spouse who cheated, a friend who blindsided you, or someone who physically, emotionally, or sexually assaulted you—essentially disregarding your humanity. Whether you're chosen last, overlooked completely, or crushed by someone important to you, rejection hurts, and it can impact the way you see yourself and the entire world around you.

Perhaps that's why it helps so much to know that you are not the only one soldiering through life wrestling with feelings of rejection. You aren't pathetic or weird. I believe an epidemic of rejection is raging in the world today, and the enemy of our souls is using it to snatch away our security and distract us from the beautiful things God has planned—a hope and a future that is good and a life filled with purpose (Jeremiah 29:11). Rejection is a normal part of life, but don't accept it as the norm in *your* life.

> *Don't accept rejection as the norm in your life.*

I always thought of myself as strong, but I remember feeling incredibly weak for allowing rejection to knock me down the way it did—ashamed, even. It took some time to realize it isn't *weakness*; it's just *human*. God created us to love. We need one another, we need acceptance, and we need community. When our needs for belonging, affirmation, and connection are not met, overcoming the pain of rejection isn't as simple as just "getting over it."

As science writer Kirsten Weir explains:

> As far as the brain is concerned, a broken heart may not be so different from a broken arm.... As researchers have dug deeper into the roots of rejection, they've found surprising evidence that the pain of being excluded is not so different from the pain of physical injury. Rejection also has serious implications for an individual's psychological state and for society in general. Social rejection can influence emotion, cognition and even physical health.... When people are chronically rejected or excluded... the results may be severe. Depression, substance abuse and suicide are not uncommon responses.[8]

Consider these other findings related to rejection:

- Researchers have found that rejection doesn't have to be direct "to trigger the brain's pain mechanism: just seeing a

picture of your ex-partner or even a video of disapproving faces activates the same neural pathways as physical pain does."[9]
- Rejection triggers inflammation in the body.[10]
- "Being on the receiving end of a social snub causes a cascade of emotional and cognitive consequences, researchers have found. Social rejection increases anger, anxiety, depression, jealousy and sadness...and can also contribute to aggression and poor impulse control...Physically, too, rejection takes a toll. People who routinely feel excluded have poorer sleep quality, and their immune systems don't function as well as those of people with strong social connections."[11]
- The implications of this epidemic of rejection can be dangerous, or even deadly. One study reported that among a group of male serial killers, 48 percent had been rejected as a child by a parent or some other important person in their lives.[12] It has been documented that the American terrorists Ted Kaczynski (aka the Unabomber) and Timothy McVeigh were tragically shaped by rejection, which played a role in their psychology and subsequent crimes.

> *Rejection is not just in your head.*

Rejection is not only in your head. It's in your body; it's in your brain; it influences your thoughts, your relationships, and your spiritual life. I remember thinking at some point along the way on my journey, *Shouldn't I be beyond this? Is it weak to admit I feel rejected?* Now I know dealing effectively with rejection isn't about progressing to a spiritual place where I never feel it; it is learning to navigate its impact in a healthier way by differentiating truth from lies and by standing on what God's Word says above all else. I can feel rejection without allowing it to rule my life.

The issue of rejection is very real for many people. It doesn't mean we're weak, spiritually immature, or bad Christians; it means we had better learn to deal with it in healthy ways. We all have buttons that Satan loves to push. I remember one evening sitting around a campfire with two dear friends and sharing our deepest thoughts—you know, those things we don't like to face or admit and only feel comfortable exposing in a very safe place. Even after years of walking with Jesus, words like *disappointed*, *rejected*, *unworthy*, *regret*, and *fear* came pouring out of the deepest recesses of our hearts. But it was not weakness; that kind of vulnerability takes strength! Together, we were openly dealing with the roots of rejection that needed to be pulled. It was healing. And one by one, as you and I and the people we walk through life with courageously bring it out into the open, we can put a stop to this epidemic.

As I've shared publicly about my experience with the impact of pornography, I've received countless messages from desperate women in similar situations crying out for help. Their stories are nothing short of heartbreaking. I grieve with these women as I read their accounts of sorrow, anger, and violation. I understand. And when they share feelings of being forsaken and hopeless, my heart tears in two. How I long to let them know that there is hope and acceptance in Jesus' unfailing love for all of us. Though I understand these feelings, the truth is they are not forsaken, and they never will be.

We must give voice to our suffering and create a safe place where it is not wasted. Because of the rejection I have experienced, I can now better relate to the pain of others than I could before the incident happened. I can make the world a better place through my acquaintance with this pain and will do whatever I can to help others in their times of need. And with God's help, I can even grow through it.

Please hear this: You are not alone. Let this book be a safe space where you can be honest and heal. As we do that together in these pages, Joyce and I invited a lovely friend to share her story.

Sarah's Story

I am now in my fifties, and as I look back over the events of my life, I sometimes feel as though a fear of rejection has become a self-fulfilling prophecy in many of my relationships. I have experienced many painful instances of abandonment and rejection, including, most recently, by the man I was married to for more than twenty years, the father of my children. I have also experienced the rupture of treasured friendships. In so many of these relationships, I have prayed, hoped, forgiven, and loved unconditionally until I am exhausted. No amount of love, prayer, hope, and effort saved me from the pain of rejection and broken relationships.

In my head, I know that God created me, that He loves me, and that through His grace, I am perfect in His sight. But there can be a wide gulf between knowing something and experiencing it, especially when we encounter pain and rejection in our human relationships throughout our lives, as all of us inevitably do.

I have thought a great deal about where my fear comes from, because I truly can't remember a time in my life when it wasn't there. I've thought about learning, at age five, that I was adopted, that I didn't come out of my mother's tummy, which meant that the person who gave birth to me hadn't wanted me and had left me at the hospital. I thought about myself as a newborn baby, being taken from my birth mother's arms in the first hours of life. I wondered how those first experiences shaped me as my senses were forming—if my first impressions of the world were as a cold, empty place, one that held no proper place for me.

When I was in fifth grade, my dad was fighting for his sobriety. I remember how much I felt like a nuisance and a burden to him and to my mom, who was trying to parent under the psychological weight of being married to a man struggling with addiction.

As I have been working through the healing process in the aftermath of my divorce, I have begun to understand two things. The first is that sometimes when we have experienced traumatic rejection at an early age, we unconsciously seek relationships with people who need us more than we need them and who need us more than they should. We do this, I think, because we so desperately long to form strong connections that do not make us vulnerable to abandonment or rejection. We think that if we are doing most of the work in a relationship, the other person is less likely to reject us. We long so very much for the security of the unbreakable connection that perpetually eludes us.

The second thing I am finally beginning to truly understand is that in this life, there is no such thing as an unbreakable connection, no such thing as a relationship that does not make us vulnerable to rejection, outside of the relationship that we have with Jesus. His is the only love that will never betray us, never abandon us, never tell us that we are not strong enough, not successful enough, not intelligent enough, not attractive enough, not good enough. As long as we continue to place our ultimate hope for unbreakable connection in other people and not in our loving, patient, and perfect God, our hopes will be dashed, sometimes devastatingly and cruelly.

As this understanding has truly begun to penetrate my heart, it has allowed me to begin to see in every relational disappointment not the inescapable repetition of an ingrained pattern of failure but another opportunity to dwell in the only safe harbor from the pain of abandonment and rejection, my perfectly loving Lord and Savior. This has also allowed me to begin to enjoy relationships without fear or the pressure of perfectionism. It has allowed me to be better at forgiving myself when I let others—and myself—down. And it has allowed me to place compassion for others and for myself above the fear of loss and the expectation that another human relationship will finally make me feel whole.

I still must continue the work I need to do to heal from past wounds and gain the tools I need to continue to grow in self-compassion and discernment about who I invite into the closest places of my heart. But understanding that the only source of unconditional acceptance is God, taking up a daily dwelling place within Him, and embracing how He transforms us from the inside—this is the truest answer to our search for ultimate belonging until we meet our Lord and Savior face-to-face.

> God's love is the only one that will not betray you.

There is hope. Yes, there is an "epidemic" of rejection overwhelming many. It can consume you, but it does not have to. With God's help, we can not only overcome the damage that has been done through rejection but also prepare ourselves to better handle what may lie ahead.

I find Psalm 27 especially meaningful for all who have experienced rejection. It serves as an important reminder that no matter who comes against you, and regardless of who may reject you, the Lord will always be there for you.

Part of this powerful psalm is below. Read it. Take it in. Read it again. I encourage you to look it up and read the entire psalm. God's Word carries healing. It is the antidote we need.

> The Lord is my light and my salvation; whom shall I fear? The Lord is the stronghold of my life; of whom shall I be afraid?...Though an army encamp against me, my heart shall not fear; though war arise against me, yet I will be confident....For he will hide me in his shelter in the day of trouble; he will conceal me under the cover of his tent; he will lift me high upon a rock. And now my head shall be lifted up above my enemies all around me, and I will offer in his tent sacrifices with shouts of joy; I will sing and make melody to the Lord. Hear, O Lord, when I cry aloud; be gracious to me and answer me! You have said, "Seek my face." My heart says to you, "Your face, Lord, do I seek."...For my father and my mother have forsaken me, but the Lord will take me in....Wait for the Lord; be strong, and let your heart take courage; wait for the Lord!
>
> Psalm 27:1, 3, 5–8, 10, 14 ESV

Lean in Closer

1. We all face rejection. With this in mind, what does this statement say to you: "Rejection is a normal part of life, but don't accept it as the norm in *your* life"?

_____

_____

2. What does the research about rejection tell you about the breadth and gravity of the pain it causes? How could these facts release you from any pressure or shame you may be carrying?

   _____
   _____

3. What, if any, physical effects of rejection have you experienced? How does your experience motivate you to work toward healing?

   _____
   _____

4. Describe how the pain of rejection may have left you feeling weaker than you'd like to be as a Christian or feeling you are "lesser" than other believers. How does knowing that this is not true help you?

   _____
   _____

5. In what ways do you relate to Sarah's story?

   _____
   _____

6. Share your thoughts and feelings about Psalm 27.

   _____
   _____

CHAPTER 5

Hope on the Horizon

Joyce

May the God of hope fill you with all joy and peace as you trust in him, so that you may overflow with hope by the power of the Holy Spirit.

Romans 15:13

After I married Dave, I spent many years surviving from day to day. I didn't have any hope of things in my life ever being different. I was unhappy, but as I mentioned, I blamed it all on someone else. One day I was praying for God to change Dave, and He stopped me in the middle of my fervent prayer and showed me that Dave was not the problem. I asked Him, "If it's not Dave, who is it?" I was shocked when He showed me it was me! Although Dave had confronted me about my behavior, I still wasn't willing to take full responsibility for it. Now God had to confront me, and He did. This left me with only two options: run away, or let God help me deal with my behavior and be willing to change. It was time to begin healing the wounds of my rejection.

At that point, God began to show me what it was like to live with me. I got angry any time I didn't get my way, and I felt sorry for myself. I regularly said things that belittled Dave, and since I wasn't happy, I didn't want him to be happy, either. Happy people irritate unhappy people. Although I knew I was not behaving well, I didn't fully realize what I was doing until God opened my eyes. When I saw the truth, I was ashamed and cried on and off for three days. I was truly repentant and ready for a new beginning.

> Happy people irritate unhappy people.

Are you in a similar place now? The new beginning I found is available to you, too.

Through reading books about abuse and how it causes rejection, I began to see that my behavior was dysfunctional. I loved the Lord, I wanted to please Him, and I began to have hope that He would heal me. As I said earlier, I thought that when I moved away from my parents' home, I had left my problems behind me.

Hope on the Horizon

I didn't realize they were still causing trouble in my soul. I was insecure, but I tried to hide it by being tough and pretending that nothing hurt me. I told myself I didn't need anyone. I didn't trust people, especially men, and I was rebellious toward Dave simply because he was a man.

I had no confidence—at least not the right kind of confidence. The confidence I did have was in myself, not in Jesus. I was bold and willing to try things, but I was also proud of any success I achieved and unaware that I desperately needed humility.

What Is Hope?

When I finally took some responsibility for my behavior, I began to feel hopeful that my life could be different. Hope is a positive attitude and mindset—a confident expectation that something good is going to happen to you at any moment. Prior to the hope God birthed in me, I had been negative about everything. My father had taught me not to trust people and not to expect anything good, and he taught me by example to be negative. He was negative, didn't like most people, found fault with everything and everybody, and was extremely critical and judgmental.

> *Hope is a positive attitude and mindset.*

The first area of my life that God began working on was my mind, in my thoughts and attitudes. I wanted the good life God promises in His Word, but my mind had to be renewed by His Word before I could have that good life.

> Do not be conformed to this world (this age), [fashioned after and adapted to its external, superficial customs], but be transformed (changed) by the [entire] renewal of your mind [by its new ideals and its new attitude], so that you

may prove [for yourselves] what is the good and acceptable and perfect will of God, even the thing which is good and acceptable and perfect [in His sight for you].

Romans 12:2 AMPC

One of the most valuable lessons God taught me was how to do my own thinking instead of just meditating on whatever fell into my mind or whatever the devil placed there. The mind is the battlefield on which the devil does war with us. He is a liar, and he works hard to deceive us by getting us to believe his lies. I believed the lie that all my problems were someone else's fault, and this kept me from dealing with my own issues. So, the wounds in my soul continued to fester, and this held me captive in a very hopeless place.

As long as I believed the enemy's lies, I had no possibility of ever being set free. God put just the right books in my hands at just the right time. I had no idea that my thoughts had power in my life. After all, they were just thoughts. But our thoughts become our words, and words become attitudes, and attitudes become actions.

Over a period of years, God renewed my mind, and I began to think according to His Word. As I did, my life changed. I had been living in darkness for years, and light was finally coming in. If your mind needs to be renewed, the fight will be fierce in the beginning. The devil doesn't easily give up ground he has gained. If you'll walk with God and be determined not to give up, then little by little you will win the battle.

> *You cannot have bad thoughts and a good life.*

If you think you can have bad thoughts and a good life, you are wrong. Or, put another way: "Where the mind goes, the man follows." My thoughts were selfish, negative, envious, critical, unforgiving, self-pitying, and fearful—so that's how my life was. But the good news is that gradually God changed me, and He can do the same for you if you are willing to face truth. He changed me by giving me a deep desire to study His Word. The more I learned about Him and about His love, kindness, forgiveness, mercy, and acceptance, the more I changed. As we look into the Word of God, we are changed into His image "from glory to glory" (2 Corinthians 3:18 NKJV).

Jesus told the people who believed in Him that if they would abide in His Word, they would know the truth and the truth would make them free (John 8:31–32). Interestingly, this is one of the first scriptures that God impressed on me when I began to really study His Word. I didn't understand it was the truth about *myself* that I would have to know to be free. God's Word is truth (John 17:17), and it is light (Psalm 119:105). Truth always exposes the darkness. Don't be afraid to let God into the secret places of your heart. He knows everything about you anyway, but He won't work until you invite Him to do so.

The Power of Faith

I then began to learn about faith and came to realize that I needed to believe what God's Word says if the promises in it were ever going to become reality in my life. For example, God's Word tells us repeatedly that we are not to fear (Isaiah 41:10; 2 Timothy 1:7; 1 John 4:18). But fear was ruling me. It would have continued to do so unless I had released my faith and learned to confront my fears by doing the very things it tried to keep me from doing. Faith is the "assurance (the confirmation, the title deed) of the things [we] hope for," and "the proof of things [we] do not see" (Hebrews 11:1 AMPC).

I began to devour God's Word, and just as food feeds the physical body and keeps it strong, God's Word is the food we need for our spiritual life. "Faith comes by hearing, and hearing by the word of God" (Romans 10:17 NKJV). I read multiple books on faith and learned how to release my faith for the healing I needed in my soul. We do that by praying, speaking faith-filled words, and taking action. Faith gave me the courage to hope for the first time in my life.

Isaiah 61:1–8 fed my spirit and kept me from giving up. It tells us that God gives us beauty for ashes, the oil of joy for mourning, and the garment of praise instead of a heavy, burdened spirit (v. 3). He makes us "trees of righteousness, the planting of the Lord, that He may be glorified" (v. 3 NKJV). It says that God will give us a "twofold recompense" (reward) for our former shame because He is a God who loves justice (vv. 7–8 AMPC).

Obedience to God

As I continued my journey, I began to realize how important obedience to God is, and I wanted to be obedient to Him. Everything God asks us to do or not to do is something that will be good for us. Even if it is hard for us to do, which it often is, it is for our good.

The Bible tells us what to do and what not to do—both in a general sense and in some specific areas, such as forgiving those who hurt or offend us (Ephesians 4:32) and using wisdom as we manage our time and money (Psalm 90:12; Proverbs 13:11). But the Holy Spirit leads us in the details of our daily life. There were times He would prompt me to apologize to Dave for something I said or did. It was hard for me to humble myself and do this, but each time I obeyed, I felt better, and it became easier to do the next time I needed to apologize. Obedience to God is "the adjustment to all inharmonious circumstances," according to the amplification of Ecclesiastes 12:13 (AMPC). The Holy Spirit is our Teacher, and He leads and guides us to the good life Jesus wants for us.

If you need help as you journey from feelings of rejection to greater strength, confidence, and the ability to trust people again, start by obeying God in even the tiniest matter, and you will be surprised at how much progress you will make.

Guilt and Shame

I had felt guilty for as long as I could remember, and it left me completely hopeless. I felt that something must be wrong with me for my father to want to do the things he did to me, and I felt that something was wrong with me because my own mother wouldn't protect me from what he was doing. Even after the abuse stopped, I felt guilty for years. I didn't always feel guilty about the abuse, but since I was rooted in guilt and rejection, I felt guilty about *something* all the time. I now know much of this was false guilt with which the devil filled my mind. I became a very legalistic Christian who tried to follow all the rules so that I didn't have to feel the guilt.

Then I discovered that although guilt is a big problem, shame is even bigger. According to the American Psychological Association's dictionary, shame is "a highly unpleasant self-conscious emotion arising from the sense of there being something dishonorable, immodest, or indecorous in one's own conduct or circumstances."[13] Simply put, when we feel ashamed, we feel embarrassed. We want to run and hide.

I was not only ashamed of what was done to me; I was ashamed of myself. I felt I should have done something about the abuse, even though I tried and nothing worked. Isaiah 61:7 says, "Instead of your shame you will receive a double portion." As I began to believe these words, I also began to trust God to free me from shame. Realizing that I had a toxic shame-based nature was a great breakthrough for me, because once I knew this, I could work toward breaking free from it. Remember, we are created by God to have confidence and be secure in His acceptance and in who we are in Christ.

As I grew, I learned how to like myself, and that made such a big difference I don't even know how to express it. I had always hated myself, but I didn't know I was trapped in self-hatred. When I began to think about my shame-based nature and started asking myself how I felt about who I was, I realized I was constantly at war with myself. I didn't like my personality; I thought it was too rough. I wanted to be sweet and kind. I wanted to be less aggressive and quieter. I wanted to be soft-spoken, but I had—and still have—a big voice. It is so deep that when talking on the phone I am often mistaken for a man. I can remember when that made me feel insecure, and I wished with all my heart I had a soft, sweet voice. Now I think it is funny, and I know that God gave me the voice I have because it is unique and catches people's attention. I can now say that I love myself in a balanced way. I'm not in love with myself, and I don't love everything I do, but I love the me that God created.

You'll find great hope in making peace with yourself and embracing all that you are, even the imperfect parts. Let God work with you to change the things He wants to change, and just accept and love the rest.

Before the Israelites could possess any of the Promised Land, God had to roll away the reproach of Egypt from them (Joshua 5:9). *Reproach* means shame, blame, guilt, disapproval, or disappointment. I believe the Israelites needed to feel good about themselves to accomplish what was ahead of them.

The Israelites were going to the Promised Land from Egypt, where they had been slaves. Even though they had been freed from Egypt, they still had a slave mentality. But God wanted them to see themselves not as slaves, but as His children—bold, strong, confident, courageous, and unafraid. The same is true for you and me. God has wonderful promises in place for us, but we must believe them, and we won't do this without knowing who we are in Christ. What does "in Christ" mean? When we accept Jesus as our Lord and believe He suffered and died to pay for our sins and the guilt attached to them, and that He rose from the dead, the Bible says we are placed in Him and He comes to live in us (Galatians 2:20). As believers, God sees us as "in Christ," and that means we have access to all the rights and privileges that Jesus has because of our faith in Him. Paul writes in Philemon 6 about the "knowledge of *every good [thing]* that is ours in [our identification with] Christ Jesus [and unto His glory]" (AMPC, emphasis mine).

Is it time to roll away the reproach of what others have done to you? To replace your shame with a double portion of God's blessing (Isaiah 61:7)? To dare to hope for something better? With Christ, all this is not only possible, but promised (Matthew 19:26).

God Uses Those the World Rejects

If you have been rejected, then you are just the person God wants to use in a special way. I think this is God's way of rewarding us for our former shame.

> *God lifts up those the world has put down.*

It also makes those who think they are something special apart from God realize that God chooses and uses whom He desires, not necessarily those who are naturally talented.

> But God has selected [for His purpose] the foolish things of the world to shame the wise [revealing their ignorance], and God has selected [for His purpose] the weak things of the world to shame the things which are strong [revealing

their frailty]. God has selected [for His purpose] the insignificant (base) things of the world, and the things that are despised and treated with contempt, [even] the things that are nothing, so that He might reduce to nothing the things that are, so that no one may [be able to] boast in the presence of God.

1 Corinthians 1:27–29 AMP

God notices those who are unnoticed by people. He uses those who have been viewed as insignificant and treated with contempt. He lifts up those the world has put down.

As I close this chapter, let me assure you that there is great hope on the horizon for you. All of God's promises are available for all people. And since He has set free people who struggle with the same things you do, He will set you free, too. Make the decision now that if anyone can be healed, you can! I can't promise you that the journey will be quick or painless, but the pain of change is much better than the pain of staying the way you are if you need healing. God says to you, "Fear not, for I have redeemed you; I have called you by name, you are mine" (Isaiah 43:1 ESV).

Lean in Closer

1. Joyce writes, "When I finally took some responsibility for my behavior, I began to feel hopeful that my life could be different." Are there areas of your life in which you also need to take some responsibility for your behavior?

2. "Hope is a positive attitude and mindset—a confident expectation that something good is going to happen to you at any moment." How does Joyce's definition of hope

encourage you? What are some glimmers of hope you have seen?

_____

_____

3. Read Isaiah 61:1–8. What promises do you see for your life in this passage?

_____

_____

4. Joyce writes, "If you have been rejected, then you are just the person God wants to use in a special way." How do you see this in 1 Corinthians 1:27–29 (AMP)? Make a list of all the potential ways God can use you. Keep it to encourage and inspire yourself during your healing process.

_____

_____

PART 2

The Lies of Rejection

The thief comes only to steal and kill and destroy; I have come that they may have life, and have it to the full.

John 10:10

CHAPTER 6

Shaped by Rejection

Ginger

*"But I will restore you to health and heal your wounds,"
declares the Lord, "because you are called an outcast, Zion
for whom no one cares."*

Jeremiah 30:17

Both Joyce and I can look back now and see clear ways rejection shaped our outlook on life and our relationships. I had no idea I would one day be so impacted by the sorrow that is caused by rejection. Perhaps you didn't think you would be either, yet here we are. Maybe I thought I was somehow immune or was more in control. I know better now. My life was shaped by this heartbreak, but God has redeemed and healed every wound. He is the Potter who molds this lump of clay into something beautiful (Isaiah 64:8).

Rejection creeps up in many ways. As a person living life in front of a television camera as I have for more than forty years, I've received a great deal of appreciation and perhaps more than a fair share of not-so-constructive criticism. Joyce certainly has, too. During one excruciatingly painful time, someone spread outright lies about me in very public ways. These were false accusations that cut me to the core and made me want to find a cave and hide away. Being the subject of speculation and of falsehoods is incredibly hard. It's difficult to remember who you truly are when all you can see is yourself through the rejecting eyes of others. In time the truth did prevail, and I learned God is indeed my vindicator (Psalm 57:2; 135:14). *Only* He determines who I am.

Rejection at the hands of family and friends is probably the most difficult. They are supposed to be your safe place. For a long time, I didn't feel accepted or welcome among some of my family members. I'm sure there was fault on both sides, but it hurt. Then my brother-in-law, whom I dearly loved, spoke words to me that brought such healing. He said he was sorry for how others in the family treated me. He bore no responsibility for it, yet made a point to apologize and tell me that he saw what was happening.

His simple words told me I wasn't alone and made me feel connected rather than rejected. He taught me the importance of noticing other people's pain. I am grateful to say that since then, those relationships have improved. It was like a door was opened for God to work in all of our hearts. What may seem like simple words can be an important moment of connection and healing.

So many of our experiences of rejection are more about what is happening inside of someone else than they are about us. When I lost a dear friend to suicide, it not only thrust me headlong into grief, but also left me reeling from shock. I felt abandoned. I was devastated and struggled with the thought that he *chose* to leave those of us who cared about him. God showed me, through this season of grief, that He is truly there for us as our Comforter (2 Corinthians 1:3). And I learned that what we perceive as rejection sometimes isn't rejection at all. It is a person in unimaginable pain dealing with something that has nothing at all to do with us.

> *What you perceive as rejection is sometimes just a person in unimaginable pain.*

And of course, there was the day when my husband's problem with pornography came to light. The confident yet somewhat naïve thirty-something-year-old me had the blinders ripped off. My greatest rejection came at the hand of the person with whom I chose to spend my life, who was supposed to have my back and my best interests in mind, the one I trusted most. My heart was shattered, and I could feel it hardening moment by painful moment.

Secret Wounds

On the outside, most people would have never known what I was going through when I found out about Tim's struggle. I continued

> A smile only hides the pain.

hosting a daily talk show, and the smile on my face hid most of the pain. But the shrapnel of exploded secrets rips open unseen wounds. They are the things almost no one knows, and we usually don't want them to see—perhaps because of shame, embarrassment, or fear. But inside, it felt like everything had changed.

The Bible tells us that secrets will come to the surface, and I believe this is for good reason.

> For there is nothing hidden that will not be disclosed, and nothing concealed that will not be known or brought out into the open.
>
> Luke 8:17

When others hurt you, even in secret, God sees it. He witnesses what happens, and He sees your pain. Though it doesn't feel good when it comes to light, the process of revealing truth is one way God protects us.

Our family once had a dog named Mr. Fitz. One day he was running in circles inside of the house, as dogs do when they have "the zoomies," when he slipped on the wood floor and fell. After this experience, he was terrified of that spot on the floor. He would stand frozen and stare at it or would give it a wide berth as he walked around it.

One day I saw Mr. Fitz stop, turn around, and literally walk backward through the spot where he had fallen. This became his answer to the problem, as if he believed that because he couldn't see it, nothing bad would happen. We can be the same with painful experiences in our lives. There are some we wish we didn't have to face, but avoiding or ignoring them does not make them untrue or go away. Joyce's mother ignored the fact that Joyce was being sexually abused, and it made everything worse. Secrets must surface so we can deal with the poison lurking beneath them. We must walk through the pain, or healing may never come.

> *Deal with the poison lurking below a secret.*

With my discovery of Tim's secret, the poison came rushing out in the form of shock, disappointment, and anger. Then came embarrassment, guilt, and fear. These are all things I would rather not have walked through, would rather not have faced at all. But had I not, I would still be there frozen on that spot, unable to move past it.

Driven by Anger

I was so incredibly angry. Angry at Tim. Angry with myself. Angry at God. Pretty much angry at the world. The anger toward Tim came first, and I must say, I was very good at it. Ephesians 4:26 says not to let the sun go down on our anger, but that was not the issue. The question was, how many full moons would come and go?

I was angry with myself because I felt weak. *How did I miss this?* I wondered. *How could I let this happen?* I felt sorry for myself, and that made me angry. It seemed unfair that when Tim revealed his secret, he felt relief. People came around him in support, but what about me? For me, the agony was just beginning.

Then I wanted revenge: *I'll show him. I am desirable, and I'll prove it.* I thank the Lord I didn't act on them, but those thoughts were dangerous territory.

Then came the anger at God. It was bad enough that my husband rejected me, but it felt as though God was rejecting me, too. "Why would You let this happen? Don't You care? What about all those prayers I prayed?" As a friend who experienced the same situation with her husband shared, "God knew what was happening and did nothing. It felt like a conspiracy."

God let me reel. He let me cry and ask and pout. I had a lot to work through, and I believe He understood that. It was the pain speaking. He didn't owe me answers, but He loved me through the questions and without returning the anger.

Eventually, I could no longer live in anger and bitterness. I was carrying so much of it I felt as though it was oozing out of my pores. I had to do something. There was too much at stake. I had two daughters who needed me. The fury inside of me was not who I was, it was not like me, and I was afraid this angry person in me would become a permanent resident. Eventually, I realized the anger wasn't working, so like a child running back to the arms of her father, I surrendered. I made the decision to release it and return to the truth of my heavenly Father's Word. There, I clung to the foundation of God's never-ending acceptance:

> I have chosen you and have not rejected you.
>
> Isaiah 41:9

> The one who comes to Me I will most certainly not cast out [I will never, no never, reject one of them who comes to Me].
>
> John 6:37 AMPC

I realized I had to release the anger I felt toward myself in order to move forward. I took to heart what the apostle Paul says about moving in the right direction in Philippians 3:13–14: "But one thing I do: Forgetting what is behind and straining toward what is ahead, I press on toward the goal."

But the anger I felt toward Tim was a different story. Overcoming that took longer—a *lot* longer. It was a long game of watching and waiting. Would he do all that he had committed to do? Could he follow through with his promises of absolute honesty, accepting accountability, and getting the help he needed? He began to seek God in a way I had never seen him do before, and when I saw him consistently fighting this battle with all his heart, hope began to sprout. And slowly, the anger began to dull.

Unexpected Guilt and Shame

I was surprised at the guilt I felt. Of course, there were changes I could make, but I did nothing wrong to cause this. Yet I couldn't help wondering: *I thought we were happy. I thought we had a good sex life. How was I so naïve? Was I not pretty enough, not desirable enough? Or was I simply not enough?*

I was so hurt, and somehow the sinking feeling crept in that perhaps I had let God down. Maybe that's why He let it happen, I reasoned. One day I was praying words I always do: "God, I love You." But then something came out of me I had never before felt the need to utter. A plea of desperation: "Please love me back." And I felt His reply so softly in my spirit as He whispered, "You *never* have to beg for my love."

With that tender answer, the guilt and shame were defeated.

Broken Trust

I didn't know how I would trust again. I am an inherently trusting person, but I am also fiercely independent, so in the beginning of our marriage, it had taken time for me to learn to give Tim more of myself. Then, after what had happened, I thought, *Look where that got me.* Had I given too much of myself away, trusted too easily? Trust, once broken, is extremely difficult to rebuild, and the impact of that breach extended beyond our marriage. I wondered,

Who can I trust? And after I had been so played, *Can I trust myself to know?*

I knew then that I had to focus on my own healing—my own heart—before I could even consider whether there would still be a marriage. My relationship with God had to come first. It was my foundation. If your trust has been broken, begin with restoring your first love. Seek first the kingdom of God and He will take care of the rest (Matthew 6:33). I sought Him above all else, and it was through my relationship with Him that I began to heal and be restored.

> *Your relationship with God comes first.*

God so gently reminded me *He* is trustworthy, *He* is faithful, *He* is steadfast, even when others are not. *He* is my strength. I love what the Bible says about how God surrounds us with His unshakable and eternal presence:

> Those who trust in the Lord are like Mount Zion, which cannot be shaken but endures forever. As the mountains surround Jerusalem, so the Lord surrounds his people both now and forevermore.
>
> Psalm 125:1–2

Mountains are magnificent reminders of God's majesty, and being in their midst always brings me peace. Psalm 121:1–2 says, "I lift up my eyes to the mountains—where does my help come from? My help comes from the Lord, the Maker of heaven and earth." I lifted my eyes to Him, and He wrapped me in His love and strength.

> *God asks you to trust Him.*

God didn't ask me to trust anyone else; He asked me to trust Him. He began helping me work through all the poison that oozed from my wounds, healing me. And I knew that I would be whole—with or without my husband.

Was I Willing to Forgive?

Eventually, when I began to think about trusting Tim again, I knew that in order to trust him, I also had to forgive him. That was a big ask. Tim was working hard and doing well, and I began genuinely trying to forgive but still felt no basis for trust. Frankly, I wasn't sure I wanted to forgive him. I'll admit, I'm getting a little angry all over again as I write, even though I forgave Tim many years ago. That's why it's vital to understand that forgiveness is a decision, not a feeling.

> *Forgiveness is a decision, not a feeling.*

The memories and triggers that spark anger don't mean I haven't forgiven. My decision is beyond my feelings, and I go back to it. The same is true with love. If I was going to stay in the marriage—and at that point I knew that was my desire—I also had work to do in my own heart. I didn't feel like forgiving; I didn't feel a lot of love at the time, but I *chose* to both love and forgive him. Eventually, the feelings followed.

Embarking on the journey of renewed trust, forgiveness, and love took time, and it is an everyday commitment. Today I know how much Tim loves me. He has proven himself trustworthy, and I love him dearly. But this is trust with my eyes open. People aren't perfect, and they can let us down. God will not.

First and foremost, when trust has been destroyed, we run to God. He is the one place where our trust is infinitely secure. As we seek Him, we receive the healing our broken hearts need.

Rebuilding Trust in Other People

For a period of time, we may place our trust in God alone. But eventually, it's important to learn to trust other people—to take that risk once again. This is a process and sometimes a painful one. Trust is precious and can be delicate, especially once broken, but it is key for any relationship to flourish, and it is a vital element of a fulfilling life. The process of rebuilding trust takes time and requires deep work on a heart level. It hinges on open communication, healthy boundaries, and accountability. I know from experience how difficult it can be, but take heart—I also know that with God's help and commitment from both parties, trust can be restored. Ask Him for wisdom and discernment, and don't be afraid to seek help.

Henry Cloud has written an entire book on this called *Trust*, and it is an extremely helpful guide to figuring out whom to trust and how to trust again after it has been damaged or broken. He writes about the "five essentials of trust," which are:

- *Understanding*, meaning that in a relationship of trust, each person needs to know and understand the other. Without understanding, trust can't take root and grow.
- *Motive*, meaning that each person is motivated by their care for the other person's good.
- *Ability*, meaning each person has the emotional resources and relational equipment needed to give and receive trust.
- *Character*, meaning that both people need to have integrity. Cloud writes, "Where there is lying, cheating, or stealing, there can be no trust. Zero."[14]
- *Track record*, meaning that people need to prove themselves trustworthy. If someone hasn't been trustworthy in the past, they shouldn't be trusted again until they have proven worthy of trust.

Cloud's book also addresses how to break our barriers to trust in several chapters under the heading "A Model for Repairing Trust." When I went through the devastation in my marriage, this book had not yet been written, but now that it has, I would encourage anyone dealing with trust issues to read and even study it.

Fighting Against Fear

As I considered learning to trust again, of course, all the what-if questions reared their ugly heads. *What if I open my heart and get hurt? What if it happens again? How can I be sure?* No one's journey is perfect, and ours has not been, either. The truth is, there are no guarantees. With one exception:

> When I am afraid, I put my trust in you. In God, whose word I praise—in God I trust and am not afraid. What can mere mortals do to me?
>
> Psalm 56:3–4

God always had my back, and He has yours. To risk trusting—to risk loving—is scary. Maybe you've tried and it didn't work. Perhaps at this point you're just numb, unable to feel much of anything at all. I get it. But life without loving others is not living at all. I refuse to live in fear of what people may do. When I get hurt again, God will be there to pick me up. People do hurt us, and relationships fail. But I chose to open my heart and trust in God because regret *is* something to fear. There are no answers to the questions that follow regret. *If only I had...Why did I...?* Don't be so afraid of rejection that you welcome regret. Instead, cling relentlessly to hope.

> *Cling relentlessly to hope.*

> We have this hope as an anchor for the soul, firm and secure. It enters the inner sanctuary behind the curtain, where our forerunner, Jesus, has entered on our behalf.
>
> Hebrews 6:19–20

Jesus will be the anchor that holds us in place through life's stormy seas. He is right there, interceding for you as the waves roll (Romans 8:34).

It's true: There was a time I didn't want to share my journey. I didn't want pornography to be my story or for Tim to be labeled. But I know now that I'm more than what happened. I am an overcomer, and so is he. Today I'm honored to tell all. I bear some scars, and they stand as reminders of God's faithfulness. But healing doesn't leave us the same. I have been shaped by rejection, but I am not defined by it. And neither are you. In fact, God has used for good what the devil meant to hurt me. He has used it to make me stronger and to help others. He molded me into a lovely new creation, and He can do the same for you.

Lean in Closer

1. How has your life been shaped by rejection?

2. In what ways have you allowed other people to shape your identity?

3. When you think about the rejection you have experienced, when was it possibly more about the other person's pain and what they were going through than it was about you?

4. What secret wounds do you carry?

5. How has anger impacted your life? Consider these areas:
    - Anger at others

       _____

       _____

    - Anger at yourself

       _____

       _____

    - Anger at God

       _____

       _____

6. How has being rejected affected your ability to trust?

    _____

    _____

7. Read Psalm 125:1–2. Ginger shared, "God didn't ask me to trust anyone else; He asked me to trust Him." How does this change your outlook on trust?

    _____

    _____

CHAPTER 7

Rooted in Rejection

Joyce

Therefore, there is now no condemnation for those who are in Christ Jesus.

Romans 8:1

If rejection begins early in life, it can become a root, meaning that the experience of rejection can be like a seed planted in the ground of a person's soul. Once the feeling of being rejected—not belonging, not feeling loved, feeling "wrong" instead of "right"—takes root in a person's life, it affects everything in some way, especially their outlook and perspective, their self-image, and their relationships with others.

Roots eventually produce fruit, and diseased roots always produce unhealthy fruit. But Jesus says that every plant that His Father did not plant will be pulled up by the roots (Matthew 15:13). In Isaiah 61, while giving hope to those who have been wounded, the prophet says, "They will be called oaks of righteousness, a planting of the Lord for the display of his splendor" (v. 3). We get uprooted and replanted in Christ. "Those who are planted in the house of the Lord shall flourish in the courts of our God" (Psalm 92:13 NKJV). What God plants will flourish and be strong like the mighty oak.

When God was uprooting the rejection I had experienced, it was painful and at times confusing. I am sure an actual plant would feel the same way if it had feelings. For the person who has been uprooted and then gets planted in Christ, it takes time to develop a new root system. It certainly took time for me.

For years, I was completely unaware of how much the rejection and the many other things I had experienced were affecting my life. I had never heard of a root of rejection, but I definitely had one. Thankfully, I have learned a great deal since that first awakening, and looking back, I can see how the root of rejection produced many negative "fruits"—negative attitudes, emotions, thoughts, and perspectives—in my life. For the rest of this chapter, I'd like to focus on the fruits of rejection in my life and how God has helped me. You may struggle with some or all of these as well, and the good news is that God can untangle the roots of rejection in your life. He can lead you into a wonderful life that bears good fruit, just as He has done for me.

Dealing with the Fruit of Rejection

1. Learn to let go of anger.

One of my big problems, which had its source in rejection, was that I wanted to control everything because I felt that if I was in control, I would be safe. At one point in my life, I had vowed that

> God has given you free will to make your own decisions.

nobody would ever tell me what to do or hurt me again, and I lived by that vow for many years. I thought I was protecting myself by making decisions that only prioritized my own needs. But making decisions this way doesn't work well in relationships, especially not in a marriage, so my controlling behavior caused problems in my relationship with Dave.

Nobody wants to be controlled. God has given us free will, and by His design we want to either make our own decisions or be included in making any decisions that affect us. Jesus has set us free (Galatians 5:1).

My controlling behavior showed up mostly in personal relationships. I could easily submit to the authority of my employer, but not to Dave or my few friends (nobody wants to be controlled by their friends!).

A major way my desire to control manifested itself was that I became angry anytime I didn't get my way. I was extremely stubborn and could stay angry for a long time. When I did this, I was simply reenacting my father's behavior. When anyone crossed my father in any way or wanted something he didn't want, his response was anger. He used his anger to control my mother, my brother, and me. I lived in fear—most often the fear of making him angry or the fear that he would abuse me again.

I carried anger into my adult life, and it was my automatic response to not getting my way. I was very selfish, but I didn't realize it. I simply thought I *had* to fight for myself, or people would mistreat me. I could not imagine anyone making a decision because they thought it would be good for me, so I determined to make decisions for myself.

I desperately needed to learn how to let go and trust God. To do that, I had to learn to stop trying to control everything. This wasn't easy, because I had been doing it all my life. Trying to control everything is hard work, and if we do so constantly, other people understandably become exhausted with us.

Gradually, God taught me to trust Him instead of trying so hard to take care of myself. Psalm 37:5 says, "Commit your way to the Lord, trust also in Him, and He shall bring it to pass" (NKJV). If we take this verse seriously and apply it to our lives, we will stop trying to control people and situations. We will learn to pray and seek God about the relationships and circumstances we are dealing with and not try to force things to happen in a certain way. We will trust God to act on our behalf, knowing He always does what is best for us. And we will wait patiently (which isn't always easy) for Him to do what needs to be done. For people who have a tendency to be controlling, this goes against their natural way of doing things. But the more we do it, the more we learn that life is much better when God is in control than when we are. I encourage you to "let the Lord lead you and trust him to help" (Psalm 37:5 CEV).

2. Live each day with joy.

Being rejected or feeling rejected takes the joy out of living. For years, I felt like I had a heaviness in my heart. I was probably depressed and didn't know it. A joyless life is a miserable life, and I had no joy. One reason for this is that a person cannot be selfish and happy at the same time.

God created us to give and serve others, not to be served (Matthew 20:28; Galatians 5:13), and Jesus Himself said, "It is more blessed to give than to receive" (Acts 20:35). I have learned that giving to others is one of the greatest blessings in the world and one that brings great joy. I have come from being totally self-absorbed to loving to give and make others happy, and I give God all the glory for this change in my life.

> Giving to others brings great joy.

There are two scriptures I think of often:

> Seek first the kingdom of God and his righteousness, and all these things will be added to you.
>
> Matthew 6:33 ESV

> Delight yourself in the Lord, and he will give you the desires of your heart.
>
> Psalm 37:4 ESV

I have learned to be joyful with simple things. There is a movie called *The Magic of Ordinary Days*, and I really like this title because I have discovered how special ordinary days can be. We often look for something spectacular to make us happy, but as we grow in spiritual maturity, we become more and more able to enjoy ordinary days and to rejoice in the Lord while we tend to

> *Learn to enjoy the ordinary in life.*

our daily routines. Most of life is ordinary, and if we cannot learn to enjoy it, we will rarely enjoy anything.

The joy of the Lord is our strength (Nehemiah 8:10). But what is the joy of the Lord? It is being glad in our hearts because of what Jesus has done for us. Although forgiving our sins is at the top of the list, He does countless other things for us, many of which we don't even notice. Think about these:

- He protects us (Psalm 121:7–8).
- He is patient with us (2 Peter 3:9).
- He is with us all the time (Psalm 139:7).
- He helps us (Isaiah 41:10).
- He loves us unconditionally (Romans 5:8).
- He accepts us and never rejects us (John 6:37).
- He heals us in our broken places (Psalm 147:3).
- He gives us hope (Jeremiah 29:11).
- And He does thousands of other things.

The Bible says that in His presence is *"fullness* of joy" (Psalm 16:11 NKJV, my emphasis). Throughout your ordinary days, think of Jesus often and, as His Word says, "make music from your heart to the Lord" (Ephesians 5:19). Try singing or just humming a tune while you work, and it will increase your joy.

I am in my eighties, and for much of my life, I have had a desire for something. But just this week I told my son David that all I want is to finish what God has called me to do with joy.

If you think about it, what steals our joy is that we want so many things and can't seem to get them. We are often jealous of others who have what we want, but we should trust God to give us what He knows is right for us to have at the right time.

Rooted in Rejection

The apostle Paul said he had learned how to be content whether he was "well fed or hungry, whether living in plenty or in want" (Philippians 4:11–12). "Godliness with contentment is great gain" (1 Timothy 6:6), and it leads to great joy.

3. Embrace hope.

As a younger woman, I was anxious much of the time because I was afraid something bad would happen to me. I had no hope, and I think this was, at least in part, due to the rejection I had experienced and the fear I had grown up with. People who have been rejected develop negative expectations, not positive ones. By the age of twenty-three,

> *Rejection develops negative expectations.*

when I married Dave, I had endured so many tragic things in my life that I could not remember ever being truly happy. I lived with a vague feeling that trouble was always just around the corner. Modern psychology calls this state of being "hypervigilance." I refer to these feelings as "evil forebodings."

> All the days of the desponding and afflicted are made evil [by anxious thoughts and forebodings], but he who has a glad heart has a continual feast [regardless of circumstances].
>
> Proverbs 15:15 AMPC

I also like this translation of the same verse:

> Every day is a terrible day for a miserable person, but a cheerful heart has a continual feast.
>
> Proverbs 15:15 GW

Eventually I was uprooted from anxiety and negativity—and replanted in hope. This process took some time. I now live with hope; it is the anchor of my soul. We must have hope before we can have faith because faith is the assurance of the things we hope for (Hebrews 11:1 AMPC). Hope expects something good to happen and is just the opposite of the evil forebodings I lived with most of my life. We could even say that hope is a positive attitude, but I was a very negative person. I thought that by not expecting anything good, I was protecting myself from being disappointed when it didn't happen.

I pray our gracious God will help you understand how much He has changed my life, and I know that He will do the same for you. However, He doesn't do it without your cooperation. He will reveal things to you and give you grace to do them, but you still must do the doing. Be prepared for a long journey, but you can enjoy it if you will celebrate each little victory with hope instead of looking at all that still needs to be done in your life.

4. Turn your focus toward others.

The fear of being rejected made me self-focused, and I believe it affects many people the same way. I thought way too much about how I looked and what people thought of me. Questions such as *Do they like me?* and *Will I be invited to their party?* ran through my head, and if I didn't get invited to the party, I felt rejected all over again. How I felt depended totally on how people treated me and what they said to me. One compliment could keep me happy for a few hours, but a negative comment or even a disapproving glance could make me miserable for days. I didn't depend on God; I depended on people to keep me happy. I was like a drug addict waiting for their next fix. A compliment, an approving glance, being included, performing a task well, or losing a few pounds—these were the types of experiences I needed to stay emotionally stable.

The problem with the kind of life I have described is that I constantly needed affirmation and acceptance from the outside because I didn't have it on the inside. I didn't know the love of God or His acceptance and approval. I didn't know the difference between my "who" and my "do." Instead of finding my value in being a child of God, I looked for it in how or what I was doing. I was exhausted all the time from working in the flesh, trying in my own strength to get all the things I needed to make me feel good, and I became angry if I didn't get them—especially if I didn't get them from Dave.

> *Find your value in being a child of God.*

Dave has always been easygoing and extremely patient, and I must admit that I took advantage of these qualities of his. Finally, after we had been married for several years, he began to confront me and told me that things had to change. He said he realized that no matter what he did, I wasn't going to be happy. Therefore, he told me, he would no longer try to make me happy, but he was going to be happy anyway and enjoy his life. When I heard these words, I was about as angry as I had ever been. I realized he meant what he said, and he was true to his word. Dave was not unkind to me, but no matter how I acted, he enjoyed his life. This was probably one of the biggest acts of love he ever committed for me. I couldn't control him anymore, and as I witnessed his joy and peace amid all my foolishness, I began to want what he had. I started getting serious about my relationship with God and wanting to change.

I believe Dave confronted me at the perfect time. Had he done it sooner, I probably would have left him. But by the time he did confront me, I had enough of God's Word in me that I knew my behavior was wrong—and I didn't want to lose Dave or live in disobedience to God.

5. Aim for accurate perceptions.

Ginger will write more about this in the next chapter, but I simply want to say here that rejection often causes our perception to be misguided or inaccurate. It can keep us from seeing things as they really are. This happens a lot in relationships when a person feels rejected.

Being misguided means having or showing faulty judgment or reasoning. We all have an imagination and some of the things we imagine need to be cast down because they are false, just as the apostle Paul teaches us to do with our thoughts.

> Casting down imaginations, and every high thing that exalteth itself against the knowledge of God, and bringing into captivity every thought to the obedience of Christ.
>
> 2 Corinthians 10:5 KJV

> *Give people what they need, not what you think they need.*

Because of the root of rejection in me, I often perceived people were rejecting me when they were not. I imagined that someone didn't like me or was ignoring me when they may have been busy or preoccupied and probably were not thinking about me at all. The more we learn to recognize and refuse to believe what is false, the better we can perceive and embrace what is true—and, according to John 8:32, that's what sets us free.

I learned an important lesson about accurate perceptions one time when I went with Dave to play golf. He wasn't playing well at all, so I patted him on the back as if to say, "It's okay." He moved my hand away and said, "Don't do that. I don't need your pity." I felt rejected and hurt because I was simply trying to comfort him. While I was seething with anger and feeling rejected, God showed me that I was giving Dave what *I perceived* he needed, but it wasn't what he *actually* needed. I was giving him what I would have needed in that situation, but he didn't need that.

Another revelation.

We often try to give others what we would need in a similar situation, but they may not need what we need. When they don't receive what we are trying to give them, we feel rejected. I can understand now that, as a man, he didn't want me to mother him in the situation on the golf course. I could have simply encouraged him and said, "You're a very good golfer. You're just having an off day."

The Roots of Rejection Can Be Pulled Up

If you have ever tended a garden, you know that some roots—the roots of weeds—need to be removed. Otherwise, healthy flowers, plants, or vegetables cannot grow. When the root of a weed has grown deep, time and effort may be required to pull it up, but it can be done.

Your life, like mine, may have been rooted in rejection. But the roots of rejection can be pulled up, and something beautiful can grow in their place. With God's help, you can identify the roots of rejection in your life and do what it takes to learn and grow in healthier soil.

Lean in Closer

1. How does Psalm 92:13 (NKJV) encourage you when it comes to pulling up the roots of rejection in your life and replacing them with God's love and acceptance?

_____

_____

2. In what ways do you attempt to use control to avoid pain?
   _____
   _____

3. How can you let go of any anger you may feel?
   _____
   _____

4. Make a list of some simple or ordinary things that could bring joy into your life:
   _____
   _____

5. Why is hope so powerful?
   _____
   _____

6. What is one way you can turn your focus away from yourself and toward someone else today?
   _____
   _____

7. Is there a situation in your life that you may not be perceiving accurately? What is it, and how could you change your perception of it?
   _____
   _____

8. Read 2 Corinthians 10:5 KJV. What misguided perceptions and negative thoughts do you need to cast down? Make a list of scriptures to combat those thoughts.
   _____
   _____

CHAPTER 8

The Lens of Rejection

Ginger

Good sense makes one slow to anger, and it is his glory to overlook an offense.

Proverbs 19:11 ESV

If you live in certain parts of the United States, you may remember that buggy period of 2024 when trillions of cicadas emerged simultaneously and overwhelmed many areas. Two different batches, the thirteen-year brood and the seventeen-year brood, hatched all at once, and it was chaos. If you live in a place that experienced the cicada apocalypse, as they called it, you likely remember. The bugs came out of the ground with only about six weeks to live, and they were ready to party, so to speak. The noise was so loud you could hardly think. The large insects flew around in random directions and smacked right into you. They were in your hair. They would fly behind the lenses of your glasses. Everywhere you went, you were intensely aware of these insects. They dominated your vision and thoughts. Then they suddenly fell and died, and their lifespan was over. After six weeks of living hard, all that was left were little carcasses all over the ground.

Dealing with rejection can be a lot like being in the middle of a cicada apocalypse. For a while, rejection is all you can see or hear, overwhelming your thoughts and expectations. But if you can shift your focus and fight back with the tools you are learning in this book, holding on to truth and to who God says you are, you'll find that eventually the noise quiets and your vision is no longer obscured. You'll be free.

If You Expect It, You'll Find It

When we experience a particularly painful rejection, or perhaps a series of dismissals and disappointments, it shapes our vision. Just as a field of vision with cicadas flying around causes us to see the world differently for a season, rejection can cause us to begin

The Lens of Rejection

to view life differently, through a lens of rejection. Joyce mentioned in the previous chapter that rejection affects every area of life, especially our outlook and perspective. Let's look a bit deeper.

You've heard of rose-colored glasses; think of this lens of rejection as the opposite. When we've sustained the wound of rejection, instead of a sunny outlook on life, the dark lens through which we see the world is one of pain and anxiety. We wonder what disappointment or experience of being overlooked or ignored we will encounter next. We begin to see and expect rejection everywhere. We even begin to imagine rejection when it isn't real. We ask ourselves:

- *What did they mean by that?*
- *Why don't they like me?*
- *Did they do that on purpose?*

When you expect rejection, you will find it. You may feel rejected by what someone said or didn't say, or what you thought they said. You may become oversensitive, and before you know it, people don't want to be around you. Or, because of the fear of being rejected, you cling so tightly to people that they feel smothered and eventually back away. You become a magnet drawing the wrong people to yourself because you are so hungry for acceptance. Jealousy grows. You always feel outside of "the circle." Friends are talking quietly, and you assume they are saying bad things about you, when they are not. You decide to reject them before they reject you, and again, you are alone.

> *If you expect rejection, you'll find it.*

As Sarah wrote in chapter 4, rejection becomes a self-fulfilling prophecy. The lens of rejection changes our perceptions, expectations, and actions. We begin to see it where it doesn't exist and make it worse where it does. Joyce and I have a beautiful friend named Mischelle, who has endured many heartaches. She shares how the lens of rejection has impacted her life.

Mischelle's Story

Rejection has been like a shadow with me my entire life. I turn and there it is, never leaving my side. I see it everywhere.

I come from a family broken by alcoholism, violence, and divorce. As a child, I felt the burden on my shoulders of helping to keep everything and everyone together. I never felt safe, treasured, or heard. Family members abused me sexually, so I was always struggling to protect myself. From there, I seemed to be constantly in a position of some guy trying something, and that shadow continued to follow me wherever I went.

Rejection shows up in our lives in different ways, though we don't always recognize it. For me, one way of trying to overshadow the rejection I struggled with was to become an overachiever. The problem with this is that when someone didn't like my work, I saw it as rejecting me, not just my idea or what I do. It was about who I am, leaving me constantly on the edge of defensiveness.

Anger was my default emotion—the bouncer at the door. I needed it to guard my heart and keep me from being hurt and misused; I needed anger to fight off the rejection. Admitting I am feeling rejected is half the battle—it feels weak, it feels broken and horrible. Now God has allowed me to recognize rejection so I can see it for what it truly is: a lie. I can see how it skews my perspective. I know anger is a protection mechanism. I know what to do with this spirit of defensiveness, so

> now I give it all to the Lord. God is my protector, and His love fully surrounds me.
>
> When it's all so damaging and shameful, the first thing you want to do is to isolate, but please don't do life alone. Be courageous, trust God, and find safe people who will listen, cry with you, and tell you the truth. No matter what, don't let go even when you want to—I wanted to. Never give up on what God can do. I now work to hold on to the truth of what God says about me instead of falling into the trap of rejection and self-pity. I have experienced God's healing, restorative love that Psalm 147:3 talks about; He is truly healing my broken heart and binding up my wounds.

Mischelle and I have spent a lot of time talking. She has also experienced the impact of pornography within her marriage. But she is learning to see life through a different filter, one that recognizes her worth and value in Christ, and one where the light of God's love overcomes the shadow of rejection.

Yearning for Connection

Viewing life through the lens of rejection, coupled with the fear of being rejected again, can make relationships challenging. It is hurtful when we desire to connect with people and it just doesn't seem to work. Developing real relationships takes time, but connection with the wrong people is worse than being alone. There are seasons in our lives when we don't have as many people alongside us as we do in others. Sometimes we have been hurt and need time to heal. At other times,

> *Developing real relationships takes time.*

God is protecting us from relationships that would not be good for us. Or perhaps He is doing something unexpected.

I remember a season when many of my friends seemed to vanish into thin air. It was a lonely time. One of my best friends wouldn't respond no matter how hard I tried to connect with her. I called and left messages. I dropped by her house, but nothing. We had been very close, and I felt terribly rejected. As I prayed about it, I realized it may not have been exactly as it appeared. Then God dropped it in my heart to stop feeling sorry for myself and to begin praying for her. Perhaps I was seeing this the wrong way. When I started praying for her, my outlook changed. I took a little gift and dropped it off at her house with a note that simply said, "I'm here if you need me." And I continued to pray.

Then one day, I heard from her, and she shared that she had been terribly depressed and couldn't reach out to anyone. She said she appreciated the note I left and was ready to talk. Through my lens of rejection, I assumed that it was all about me when, in reality, she was in desperate pain. She needed the support of a true friend: love, prayer, and patience, rather than offense. Today, many years later, she is still one of my dearest friends.

During that time, God also showed me that I had become more dependent on my friends than I was on Him. Rather than clinging to rejection and sensitivity, I needed to draw closer to God. In that season, I took my cares and hopes and dreams directly to Him, without the filter of anyone else's perspective, and my relationship with Him grew in beautiful ways. I experienced James 4:8 in action: "Draw near to God and He will draw near to you" (NKJV). Sometimes God needs to get our attention because He wants to do something wonderful in our lives. With time, my friends worked their way through the busy seasons, distractions, and challenges of their own, and again I enjoyed those relationships. I cherish my friends, but I carry that priceless lesson with me still today.

Expect the Best

One of the best ways to knock off rejection-colored glasses is this: Rather than expecting to be hurt, choose to expect the best. Expect good things from God and from people. Give others the benefit of the doubt. When I committed to doing this many years ago, my outlook changed, and my world became a happier place. Philippians 4:8 teaches us, "Finally, brothers and sisters, whatever is true, whatever is noble, whatever is right, whatever is pure, whatever is lovely, whatever is admirable—if anything is excellent or praiseworthy—think about such things." Don't look for the worst; look for the beauty. Try it, and watch your hope and joy grow!

> Choose to expect the best.

True, you will be disappointed at times. I certainly have been. People do not always do what is best. But I would rather expect the best and be disappointed sometimes than always be prepared for the worst and live under the looming shadow of suspicion and doubt. Why focus on what may not happen at all? Now and then we will be hurt, but that is still better than looking for the worst, because when we do that, we tend to find it. We may even draw it out of people. I would rather expect the best and be happy—not gullible or delusional but walking in the joy God promises rather than dread of what someone else's next action or decision might bring. And I've found that when I expect the best, I get it most of the time.

I encourage you to choose to love as Paul describes in 1 Corinthians 13:7: Love "bears all things, believes all things, hopes all things, endures all things" (NKJV). Love believes the best of others and hopes or expects the best to happen. Cultivating this outlook was revolutionary for me. Try it and see what it does for you.

You may wonder what Paul meant by "Love bears all things"

and "endures all things"—I certainly did. Does it mean we have to put up with anything and be a doormat? Is a woman who is being abused meant to endure it, or is someone whose spouse is cheating on them supposed to simply bear it? Not at all. I've learned that it means love is strong. It cares enough to confront difficult issues, set boundaries, and love as Jesus does when we face hard times. It doesn't mean we stay in dangerous situations or must live with wrongdoing. It does mean that God's love—a bigger love than romantic love—can endure even after we've been hurt. His kind of love cannot be defeated.

Just Try to Offend Me

> *Refuse to be offended if someone tries to hurt you.*

The harder we are to offend, the less we will grapple with rejection. It's fun to refuse to be offended when someone is attempting to hurt you. It frustrates them, and I'll admit I enjoy that. It takes the power away from them and puts it in God's hands, because that's where we are placing our trust.

Try to be unoffendable. There is great benefit in choosing to let it go. Remember, you won't be everyone's cup of tea. Some relationships aren't meant to be. I once hired an assistant, and I felt that things were going well. But after a few weeks, she came to me and said it wasn't working for her. She didn't think our personalities were meshing. Ouch! At first, I was a little offended. It was a great job. I'm so much fun to work with. What was she not seeing? But in the end, I sent her off with a blessing and chose to see it as part of life, not rejection. She was happier, and my next assistant was the perfect fit.

It's important to say here that there are times when we need to

The Lens of Rejection

take a stand. Being difficult to offend does not mean we accept improper situations or injustice. Jesus was extremely disturbed by the people who were misusing His Father's house, the temple, and He tossed them out (Matthew 21:12–13). When Tim brought pornography into our house, I didn't say, "You know what? It's fine. I choose not to be offended." That is not God's definition of love toward Tim or toward me. It was bad for our family, it was bad for him, and something had to be done. But even in such situations, we have a choice. We can continue to soak in the offense, or we can find a way to change our lens and focus on what is needed to move forward.

Be prepared. Being difficult to offend doesn't come naturally. It takes commitment—and practice. It requires a change in the way we think and, most of all, supernatural help. Ask the Holy Spirit to lead you in this and He will; He certainly has led me. And remember, you aren't perfect, either. Give people the same mercy you would want them to give you. These next two scriptures continue to help me in my journey to become unoffendable and love others. I pray they will help you too:

> *Remember that you aren't perfect, either.*

> Do not pay attention to every word people say, or you may hear your servant cursing you—for you know in your heart that many times you yourself have cursed others.
> Ecclesiastes 7:21–22

> Be completely humble and gentle; be patient, bearing with one another in love. Make every effort to keep the unity of the Spirit through the bond of peace.
> Ephesians 4:2–3

Refuse offense. Don't take it personally. Instead, release all those things you hold so tightly in every area of your life into God's loving hands. Regardless of what people may say or do, you can let it go when you trust that it is He who holds and cares about it all:

- Your relationships
- Your reputation
- Your success
- Your future
- Your heart

Talking Yourself off the Ledge

There are times when our feathers are ruffled, our filter of rejection is turned on full power, and we want to explode. Before you do that, take a step back and consider doing these things:

- View the situation logically rather than through the lens of rejection. Ask, *Is this rejection real or perceived? Am I possibly being more sensitive because of the wounds I have experienced?*
- Believe the best. Perhaps you don't have all the facts. Maybe there are extenuating circumstances.
- Remember that the more you love someone, the more they can hurt you, sometimes without meaning to. Maybe what the person did or said was unintentional.
- Ask yourself, *Am I being difficult to offend? Is this worth upsetting my life over? Can I choose to let this one go?*
- And remember, the other person sees life through *their* filter of hurt and pain. The situation may have little to do with you. The lens they view you through may be colored by their upbringing, beliefs, current circumstances, or rejections.

Now is the time to take off those rejection-colored glasses. Remember the questions I began with?

- What did they mean by that?
- Why don't they like me?
- Did they do that on purpose?

Let me tell you this: It really doesn't matter. You will likely never know the answers to these questions. You are not responsible for other people's motives, only for how you respond. It's time to stop caring about what people think and to simply *care* about people. When you do experience the pain of rejection and offense, God will care for your heart.

> *Stop caring about what people think and simply care about people.*

Lean in Closer

1. How might you be seeing through a lens of rejection?

2. In what ways do you relate to Mischelle's story?

3. Read Philippians 4:8. How does it describe "expecting the best"?

4. What does this statement mean to you: "The harder we are to offend, the less we will grapple with rejection"? How will you work toward becoming difficult to offend?

5. Write out your plan to "talk yourself off of the ledge." Keep it in mind, and practice it when feelings of rejection rise up.

CHAPTER 9

Walls of Protection

Joyce

No longer will violence be heard in your land, nor ruin or destruction within your borders, but you will call your walls Salvation and your gates Praise.

Isaiah 60:18

When people have been severely rejected, they try to find ways to protect themselves so they won't feel the pain of being devalued, ignored, wounded, or excluded again. They may even do this without realizing it. One way they try to protect themselves is to build walls, symbolically, around themselves—ways of relating that will keep other people from getting too close to them.

Walls are built for protection. Some people build walls around their homes. Ancient cities and towns had walls around them to protect them from their enemies. When someone hurts me, I can feel invisible walls go up between us. I erect those walls, and only I can take them down. The wall might be a fear of being hurt again, and it can only come down through courage. The wall could be anger, and it can only be torn down through forgiveness.

When we wall others out of our lives, we wall ourselves in. We imprison ourselves in isolation, thinking we will prevent ourselves from being hurt, but we are doing just the opposite. You may shut someone out of your life, but then you are lonely. As believers in Christ, we are part of His body. The church is called the body of Christ, and each individual part is needed and important. When one part of the body (one person) gets hurt and chooses to withdraw, it affects the whole body.

> *When you wall people out, you wall yourself in.*

God showed me a good example of this one day when I stepped on one of my feet with the other foot. Immediately I withdrew my aching foot and began to rub it with my hands. When one part of the body hurts, other parts come to the rescue. Eventually I had to put my foot back on the floor and start walking again. Life works the same way when someone hurts us. We may automatically withdraw initially, but eventually we must get involved again or we cannot function properly.

When my foot was injured, if I had said, "I will never let my foot get involved again because I don't want it to get hurt," it would be foolish. None of us would do that, and neither should we withdraw from our church family or our natural family and friends when we get hurt emotionally. If we are involved with people, we risk being hurt. We get hurt and we hurt people. This is part of being in relationships. We get hurt, we forgive, and we get involved again.

I once heard that an average toddler, twelve to nineteen months old, falls about seventeen times per hour while learning how to walk. That is well over a hundred times a day! I was shocked because my children didn't seem to fall that much, but perhaps they did. Toddlers fall, get hurt, and sometimes cry, but then they get up and try again. I have a great-grandson who is just learning to walk. My daughter told me that he walks until he falls, and then he crawls again for a while before he gets back up and starts walking. In other words, he withdraws from walking for a while but always gets involved again.

Perhaps you have been badly rejected at some time and have withdrawn from a place or a person—or even from life. If so, I greatly encourage you to get involved again. You are hurting yourself more than you are hurting the person or people who hurt you. Obviously, I am not suggesting you get involved with someone who has been abusing you. You have a right to protect yourself from that kind of treatment.

Inner Vows

Each time I was rejected or hurt by other people, I made a vow in my heart that they would never do it again. I determined that

> *Open your heart and let people in.*

no man would ever tell me what to do again after years of being controlled by my father. I determined that I would never get close enough to anyone to let them hurt me, so I always kept people at what I thought was a safe distance. I didn't open my heart and let anyone in. I had relationships, but never close ones. There was always a part of me that I kept closed off. Although I didn't realize it at the time, living this way wasn't good for me and certainly wasn't God's will for my life.

To be completely healed, I had to break those inner vows. You might say I had to come out of hiding, and although it was frightening, I had to open my heart to people and trust that when I got hurt, God would heal me. Have you made any inner vows that need to be broken? Once you've identified any inner vows you may have made, simply pray and repent for making them, and ask God to release you from them and help you trust Him to do what needs to be done in your life.

Stop Pretending

One way we often try to protect ourselves from rejection is to pretend that nothing hurts us. We send the message "You can't hurt me because I don't care." If someone says "I'm sorry if I hurt you," we might lie, act tough, and say "You didn't hurt me." But this would not be true. The psalmist David says that God desires "truth in the inner being," and he prays, "Make me therefore to know wisdom in my inmost heart" (Psalm 51:6 AMPC).

If someone hurt me, I would say to myself, *Who needs you? I can make it on my own.* We are created to work together, to need one another and participate together—and all the pretense in the world won't change this. Our strength is multiplied ten times when we work together. As Deuteronomy 32:30 teaches us, with

God's help, one person can put a thousand to flight and two can put ten thousand to flight. It is important to be truthful, because when we lie to other people, we also lie to ourselves. It's much better for us to speak the truth to ourselves and to others, and to live in love as we do it:

> *When you lie to others, you lie to yourself.*

> Let our lives lovingly express truth [in all things, speaking truly, dealing truly, living truly]. Enfolded in love, let us grow up in every way and in all things into Him Who is the Head, [even] Christ (the Messiah, the Anointed One).
>
> Ephesians 4:15 AMPC

Pretending nothing could hurt me caused me to feel I always had to be strong. I felt I had to be the one to take responsibility, the one to fix everything. This was exhausting, and eventually the stress of it began to show up in my body and emotions. No one can be strong all the time; occasionally we need to say "I can't do it." We can do anything God wants us to do, but not everything everyone else wants, or even all we want to do.

I recently realized that anytime I asked a Christian how they were, they almost always said "Fine." I knew that couldn't possibly be the case all the time, and I determined that I am going to tell the truth. If I have a headache, I will say "My head hurts, but I'm trusting God that it will get better." If I am tired, I will say "I am tired but expecting God to energize me."

I once preached a message on this, encouraging people to be real with one another and not pretend everything was great if it isn't. I want people to pray for me, and they can't do it effectively if I don't tell them the truth about what is going on. There may be some people we don't want to share with, but at least we should say "I'm dealing with something, but God is helping me." If they push to find out what it is, we can simply say we don't want to talk about it.

Being truthful, especially with ourselves, is very important. I read recently that spiritual integrity is the ability to be brutally self-honest. Do you really know yourself, or are you afraid to take an honest look? One way to get to know a lot about yourself is to check your motives for what you do to see if they are pure. Let's ask ourselves, *Am I doing something just to keep someone from rejecting me or becoming angry with me? Or do I truly believe I should do it? Am I doing something to be well thought of, or because I believe it is the right thing to do?*

Let's stop any pretending, be real, and decide to be honest always. We can tell the truth yet avoid being negative. Telling people that you feel bad could be considered negative, but saying "I don't feel very well, but I believe God's healing power is working in me, and I expect to feel better soon" is telling the truth in a positive, constructive way.

Self-Defense

Self-defense is another wall we build to try to protect ourselves from the pain of rejection. Anytime someone hurts us or says something negative about us, we may be tempted to put up walls by verbally defending ourselves because we want them to believe we are a good person. Such conversations often end in heated arguments and more hurt feelings.

Sometimes when our walls go up because we feel rejected by a person, we think, *I will make you more miserable than you are making me.* But God is our Vindicator, and He wants us to trust Him to make wrong things right. He is our Protector and our Comforter. First Corinthians 13:5 says that love "keeps no record of wrongs" we have suffered. The best course of action is to forgive the person who hurt you and let God take care of it. I know this isn't always easy, but God's grace will help us do it if we are willing. Or, when someone hurts me, I may decide to sit them down and correct them, so they know how to treat people right. As a teacher, I have had to learn when and where my gifts should operate—and when I am trying to do something that God hasn't asked me to do. If someone treats us wrong and we forgive and pray for them instead, God as our Vindicator will take care of the situation. He may not do it the way we want Him to or when we want Him to, but He will do it.

> *Forgive people who hurt you.*

Have you noticed that Jesus never tried to defend Himself no matter what people accused Him of? Instead, He entrusted Himself and everything to God, who judges fairly (1 Peter 2:23). When we trust God completely and get busy doing His work instead of striving to protect ourselves, we will find that we notice less and less rejection because we are not focused on how people make us feel.

If you are tempted to defend yourself, I want to remind you that the Holy Spirit is your Advocate. This means He functions like an attorney, and He will plead your case. It is not your job, so let Him be your defense.

Trying to Buy Protection from Rejection

I know a woman who has a deep root of rejection and is extremely insecure. She frequently buys gifts for people, but she does it to buy their friendship. Her gifts come with strings attached. When we give, we should give freely, without expecting anything in return.

When someone does pay attention to this woman, she suffocates them because she is so starved for love and affection. She never got these things from her husband, who regularly cheated on her with other women and was abusive to her physically and verbally. I certainly feel for her, but she doesn't see what she is doing. She truly believes she is giving gifts because she is a nice person. She even frequently talks about how much she does for others.

Make sure this type of behavior is not a pattern in your life.

I once wanted to become part of a certain group of people at a church I attended. For that to happen, I had to be liked by a specific woman. Otherwise, I was not getting into the group. I bought her affection with compliments and gifts, and I did get into the group, just as I thought I wanted. But in the end, these were the first people to reject me when God called me to teach His Word. Always remember that if you get a friend by buying them, you will have to keep doing it to maintain their friendship. This kind of behavior is not pleasing to God, because He wants our motives to be pure.

Self-protection and other means of evading rejection seem to make sense when we've been hurt, but they are fraught with pitfalls. Wanting to defend yourself against pain is natural, but beware of the problems it can cause. Instead, I encourage you to begin to trust God to be your protector and ask the Holy Spirit to lead you each step of the way. When you do, I can promise that you will be a healthier, happier person.

Lean in Closer

1. How does Isaiah 60:18 AMPC redefine protection for you? It says: "Violence shall no more be heard in your land, nor devastation or destruction within your borders, but you shall call your walls Salvation and your gates Praise."

_____

_____

Walls of Protection

2. Joyce writes, "When we wall others out of our lives, we wall ourselves in." How have you seen this at work in your life?

   _____
   _____

3. Joyce observes that in relationships, "We get hurt, we forgive, and we get involved again." Why is getting involved again important?

   _____
   _____

4. What are some examples of the walls of protection mentioned in this chapter that you need to tear down?
   - Inner vows

     _____
     _____

   - Pretending to be fine

     _____
     _____

   - Deflecting the pain

     _____
     _____

   - Defensiveness

     _____
     _____

   - Buying relationships

     _____
     _____

5. What additional walls of protection might you have built around yourself that need to be torn down?

   _____
   _____

CHAPTER 10

Perfection and Rejection

Joyce

Not that I have now attained [this ideal], or have already been made perfect, but I press on to lay hold of (grasp) and make my own, that for which Christ Jesus (the Messiah) has laid hold of me and made me His own.

Philippians 3:12 AMPC

God calls us to perfection (Matthew 5:48), but His Word also tells us we will be working toward it as long as we live on the earth (Philippians 3:12). Matthew 5:48 in the Amplified Bible, Classic Edition, helps us understand this:

> You, therefore, must be perfect [growing into complete maturity of godliness in mind and character, having reached the proper height of virtue and integrity].

God has shown me there are two pathways to perfection: the illegal way and the legal way. The illegal way is striving to perfect ourselves by pleasing everyone, becoming a workaholic to try to prove we can succeed, and trying so hard to be just right that we exhaust ourselves. The legal way is to accept the Perfect One, Jesus Christ, as your Lord and Savior. When you do, He makes you the righteousness of God in Him (2 Corinthians 5:21). He washes you in His blood, He cleanses you, and He forgives all your sins and remembers them no more (Hebrews 8:12; 1 John 1:7 AMPC). You are perfect in His eyes. He sees you as a finished product, and you will be exactly as He planned before sin entered the world. He is not angry that you have not arrived at the place of perfection in your daily life. All He wants is for you to keep pressing on to be more like Him, loving Him, and receiving the love and acceptance He has for you.

God has promised to change us in the twinkling of an eye when Jesus returns to take us to heaven with Him (1 Corinthians 15:52). This means that whatever is still lacking in us will be completed at that time.

> And I am convinced and sure of this very thing, that He Who began a good work in you will continue until the day of Jesus Christ [right up to the time of His return], developing [that good work] and perfecting and bringing it to full completion in you.
>
> Philippians 1:6 AMPC

We should all press toward the goal of spiritual maturity, and we should be able to see ourselves making regular progress through the work of the Holy Spirit in our lives. But as flawed people, we will always make mistakes. Perfection sounds great, and when we've faced rejection in our lives, we must be careful not to fall into the trap of trying to be perfect in order to gain acceptance.

Will Perfection Protect Me from Rejection?

We should not strive to be perfect or achieve perfection to avoid rejection or to cause others to think well of us. We should do everything as though we are doing it for the Lord, not to get things from people or to think we can obtain God's favor by never making mistakes. No matter how hard we try to be perfect on our own, it won't work, and we may find ourselves rejected anyway.

A perfectionist, generally speaking, is someone who refuses to accept anything short of perfection. Perfectionists require that they do everything flawlessly. They feel they must be without fault, and they typically demand the same from others. Some people try to earn acceptance through perfection. *After all,* they think, *if I am perfect, what can you possibly find wrong with me? You must accept me if I do everything right. That way, I'll be accepted, not rejected.*

Perfectionism is the tendency to place unrealistic demands on oneself or other people. Common traits of it include fear of failure, self-criticism, obsessive thinking, seeking reassurance, setting unattainable goals, and thinking negative thoughts about yourself for mistakes or failures.

People who have been rejected and still carry the pain of it often revert to perfectionism so they will not have to endure the pain of rejection again. The pain of rejection is so intense that, as I have mentioned, we often build systems to protect ourselves from it. Perfectionism is one of them. But perfection comes with a price. When we seek to be perfect or to perform flawlessly, we will always end up disappointed because we are trying to reach a goal that is unattainable. Even if we could be perfect, some people would still reject us because they would resent our perfection. Others would reject us because of *their* issues and insecurities, not ours.

We All Have Weaknesses

For years, I tried hard to be perfect and to always be strong. I remember the day God whispered in my heart, "Joyce, it is okay for you to have weaknesses." I felt as though a thousand pounds had been lifted off my shoulders. No one tries to have weaknesses, but we all have them. We have both strengths and weaknesses. God wants us to use our strengths and trust Him to be strong through our weaknesses. Even the apostle Paul had a weakness he referred to as "a thorn in my flesh" (2 Corinthians 12:7). Let's look at what he said about this in 2 Corinthians 12:7–10:

> Therefore, in order to keep me from becoming conceited, I was given a thorn in my flesh, a messenger of Satan, to torment me. Three times I pleaded with the Lord to take it away from me. But he said to me, "My grace is sufficient

for you, for my power is made perfect in weakness." Therefore I will boast all the more gladly about my weaknesses, so that Christ's power may rest on me. That is why, for Christ's sake, I delight in weaknesses, in insults, in hardships, in persecutions, in difficulties. For when I am weak, then I am strong.

Some Bible translations call Paul's thorn in the flesh "a messenger of Satan." No one seems to be sure what the thorn was. Some think it was the difficulties that Paul experienced because of his ministry; others believe it was a physical ailment or may have been a person who was an annoyance to him. This thorn was given to Paul to keep him from being conceited because of the "great revelations" God had given to him (v. 7). Whatever the thorn was, it is obvious that God viewed it as a weakness, and He refused to remove it even though Paul asked Him three times to do so (vv. 8–9). God told Paul that His grace was sufficient, and that His power would be made perfect in weakness (v. 9). Paul said that he would boast about his weaknesses so that the power of Christ might rest upon him (vv. 9–10).

Hebrews 4:15 teaches us that we have a high priest who can sympathize with our weaknesses. This scripture and others about human weakness relieve us of the pressure to be perfect all the time (Matthew 26:41; Romans 8:26, 15:1). We all want to do the best we can, but if we could behave perfectly and never hurt anyone, there would be no need for the Bible to include teaching on forgiveness. Yet it speaks to us about receiving forgiveness from God (Psalm 103:12; Ephesians 1:7; 1 John 1:9) and extending it to others (Matthew 6:14; Ephesians 4:32; Colossians 3:13).

Life is wonderful when you look at the joys and good things you have experienced, but if you focus only on the pain you have endured, it may seem like pain is all there is to life. Trying to keep yourself from suffering the pain of rejection or other hurts is harder work than simply dealing with difficult or painful situations as they arise.

When people mistakenly think they are perfect, they may become prideful and judge people who don't do things the way they do. A perfectionist is insecure, and they try to prove they are valuable through being perfect. If they demand perfection not only from themselves but also from the people around them, they are impossible to please and will experience more rejection because of the pressure they put on themselves and others.

Do What's Right and Pray for Those Who Hurt You

If you want people to love you, show them mercy and do all you can do to help them feel good about themselves. Don't be demanding and critical of every tiny mistake they make. We can't make people love us, but we can treat them well even if they have hurt us. Each of us is only responsible before God for our actions, not for anyone else's. The merciful will receive mercy (Matthew 5:7). I encourage you to decide that you will do what is right no matter what anyone else does.

> *Why worry about what other people think of you?*

Most people who develop ways of trying to protect themselves from rejection don't even realize what they are doing. I didn't, and each time God showed me another way I was trying to protect myself, it took a little more pressure off. But it was also hard to give up my self-protective mechanisms.

Why do we worry so much about what people think of us? Their thoughts can't hurt us. Words can hurt us, but only if we give them permission to do so. Do you think Jesus ever worried or was the least bit concerned about what people thought of Him, what people said about Him, or how they would judge Him?

> He was despised and rejected by mankind, a man of suffering, and familiar with pain. Like one from whom people hide their faces he was despised, and we held him in low esteem...He was oppressed and afflicted, yet he did not open his mouth.
>
> Isaiah 53:3, 7

Jesus understands rejection; He knows how you feel. Let Him be your example of how to behave when you are rejected. It may not be easy, but it is the only way that works. He continued to love and forgive people no matter how they felt about Him (John 13:1; Luke 23:34). If people rejected Him, He felt bad for them because they were missing out on the truth that would make them free.

If you can manage to have the good opinion of yourself that God has of you, then when people reject you, instead of becoming angry with them, you can simply think they missed out on having a good friend. I watch how Dave reacts if anyone ever rejects him, and he simply says, "That's between them and God; it is not my problem." And I am sure he doesn't give the situation another thought.

Jesus was perfect, and people still rejected Him (John 1:11). So even if you could manage perfection, it doesn't guarantee that some people will not reject you.

As I mentioned earlier, it seems that rejection is on the rise—both Ginger and I would go so far as to call it an "epidemic"—so it's obvious that it is a major issue in society today. A few years ago, I read the statistic that 10 percent of people won't like us no matter what we do. But I recently read that now 25 percent, or one out of every four people, will reject us no matter what we do.[15] The world we live in today is full of angry people, and many of them don't even know what they are angry about. If you happen to be around when they are angry, you just might become a convenient person for them to take their anger out on.

The world is full of pressure, confusion, and fear. People know things are not right, but they don't know why unless they know Jesus. In addition, they are frustrated because they don't know how to fix the problems they see. The Bible tells us that in the last days, prior to Jesus' return, things in the world will get very bad and that people will behave in terrible ways (Matthew 24:3–12; 2 Timothy 3:1–5, 13). Our job is to pray for them and do our best to represent Jesus through behaving the way He wants us to.

Be Yourself

If you are going to be free to be yourself, then you absolutely cannot be worried about whether or not people like you. If you trust God, He can give you two people who love you for every one who doesn't. When Dave and I were asked to leave our church and I lost most of my friends, I was lonely for a long time. But that is not the case now. God has more than made it up to me. He has given me honor to replace the shame and many open doors to replace the one that was closed to me. Trust God, and He will give you back more than you lost.

> God will give you back more than you lost.

Being yourself and not pretending to be what you think everyone wants you to be is one of the best things you can do for yourself. I tried to be like so many people in order to be accepted that I reached a point where I didn't know who I was anymore. I tried to be like Dave, who was always calm. I tried to be like my friend, who was very talented. She played the guitar and sang, made her family's clothes, grew and canned vegetables, made jelly, and did many other creative things, while I did well just to sew a button on and make it stay. I tried to be like my pastor's wife, who was sweet, patient, and submissive, and that didn't work for me, either. God wouldn't help me be someone else because He created me to be myself. I needed some polishing, but He would do that in good time.

I believe I can say now that I am who God made me to be. I still have a few rough edges, and God is working on them. But I'm open, straightforward, and willing to share my faults. I am not a quitter—I am very determined! I love to give, and I really want to help people find healing, through Jesus, of the things that have hurt them in life. I am also impatient, a little controlling, a bit selfish, and judgmental at times. I am complete in Christ (Colossians 2:10), and God is working out of me what He has worked in me. I'm still a project under construction, but God is my architect, so I am content to let Him work. And I'll enjoy my life while He does. One day, we shall see Him face-to-face, and we shall be like Him (1 John 3:2). But until then, we anxiously await the glorious day of His return when His work in us will be truly complete.

I'm now in my eighties and I'm still going strong, leaning on God every step of the way. I work out with weights and a trainer three times a week, I get tired more than I once did, and I've had to learn how to navigate change, because only a fool thinks they can always do what they have always done.

I'm at a place in life where I could retire and do anything I want to do. But I only want to do what I am doing. If God ever retires me, I will still be Joyce Meyer, and God will still love me. Always remember that God doesn't love you because of what you do; He loves you because you are His son or daughter. He certainly doesn't expect perfection from you. He knows you can't be perfect. He didn't create you to be perfect; He created you to depend on Him, and He won't ever reject you because of shortcomings or imperfections. Instead, He rejoices over you and He delights in you (Zephaniah 3:17).

God has done so much for me in my fifty years of serving Him that I can't even remember all of it. I'm like the blind man who was healed by Jesus (John 9:1–6). Religious leaders kept questioning him about his healing, and he finally says, "One thing I do know. I was blind but now I see!" (John 9:25).

I want you to know and believe that God is waiting to work in your life. The Holy Spirit is your Comforter and Counselor (John 14:26 AMPC), so feel free to take any problem you have to Him, and He will guide you in knowing how to solve it. He will heal your wounds from rejection and any other pain that you have. Jesus said, "Come to me, all you who are weary and burdened, and I will give you rest" (Matthew 11:28).

Are you suffering under the lie that you are flawed, that you are not good enough, that something is wrong with you? Have you come to believe that if only you work hard enough, people will accept you? If so, then remember the two pathways to perfection: the legal way and the illegal way. Choose the legal way, and realize that despite your human imperfections, because of the finished work of Christ, God views you as perfect. You'll continue to grow in maturity, but you can rest assured that Jesus has already attained perfection, and that because you are in Him, God doesn't see your shortcomings. He sees you through the perfection of His Son, and He accepts you unconditionally.

Lean in Closer

1. Would you call yourself a perfectionist or say you have perfectionistic tendencies? In what ways might you be hiding behind perfectionism to avoid rejection or prove your value to yourself or to others?

   _____

   _____

2. Joyce shares, "We have both strengths and weaknesses. God wants us to use our strengths and trust Him to be strong

Perfection and Rejection

through our weaknesses." List some of your strengths and weaknesses. How can God use your strengths for His glory, and how can you receive His help for your weaknesses?

3. Hebrews 4:15 says that Jesus sympathizes with our weaknesses. How does this biblical truth release you from the pressure to be perfect?

4. Who has hurt you, and why is it important to pray for them?

5. What does the statement "Jesus was perfect, and people still rejected Him" mean to you?

6. Why is it true that "Being yourself and not pretending to be what you think everyone wants you to be is one of the best things you can do for yourself"?

PART 3

The Pathway to Healing

Don't run from suffering; embrace it. Follow me and I'll show you how.

Matthew 16:24 MSG

CHAPTER 11

Reject the Lies of Rejection

Ginger

We demolish arguments and every pretension that sets itself up against the knowledge of God, and we take captive every thought to make it obedient to Christ.

2 Corinthians 10:5

If you can make someone believe the right lies, you can potentially get them to do anything you want. Satan is a liar and a deceiver (John 8:44), and he loves it when we have been rejected because he can press in and, through his lies, make us feel even worse about ourselves than we already do. He knows that after we've been used, abused, and abandoned, he can use some old-fashioned mind games against us to throw us further off course. When we are already off-center and isolated, there's no better time to use more lies to change the way we see the world around us, destroy our confidence, and potentially thwart our God-given purpose.

I began my story in chapter 3, describing how my husband's rejection hit me like a "screaming indictment of everything I was not, evidence of my unworthiness, and a huge 'I told you so' from latent insecurities looking for a chance to surface." This is a vivid and painful description of some of the lies rejection tells us, and the shocking thing is, I had no idea those thoughts were lurking deep inside me. When I thought I could no longer trust what I believed to be true because of what I learned about Tim's betrayal, the enemy had a field day. Rejection whispered in my ear, "You're unwanted, unloved, unworthy," and I took the bait.

> *Rejection loves to lie to you.*

Rejection loves to lie to us. Has it ever lied to you? Maybe it has caused you to think or say to yourself:

No one cares about me.

It's all my fault.

I will never be truly accepted.

Lying thoughts such as these can be especially overwhelming at night when you're in bed trying to sleep. The racing questions

What did they mean by that? Why did they do that? and the conversations play over and over again in our heads. This is the battleground; this is when you fight back! Pray against the tentacles of those thoughts. Don't allow them to wrap around your heart and take root, enabling them to grow into full-on rejection. It is vital that you become determined to recognize truth over lies. A thought that drops into your head is not the problem; the real danger is when you allow those thoughts to turn over and over again in your mind and make a home there.

Beat Rejection at Its Own Game

We've said it's not a matter of *if* rejection will come; it *will*, so be prepared. You get to choose how you will respond and how much power you will allow it to have over your life. It is a matter of separating the lies that rejection bombards you with from the truth of God's Word—of separating the truth of who you are from the accusations that rejection wants you to accept. And then you must firmly stand your ground.

Here is the strategy: We will learn to recognize the ploys of rejection, beating it at its own game, and take those lying thoughts captive (2 Corinthians 10:5). It's time to take a strong stand and refuse to allow rejection to take root. We can reject the rejection that is working to derail our joy, our confidence, and our purpose!

> *You can reject rejection.*

We can determine to fight relentlessly against the seeds of anger, mistrust, and insecurity that the enemy is working to plant in our lives. God has helped me discern and refuse the lies of rejection and put an end to the mind games the enemy loves to play, and I've seen the difference this has made in my life. He has walked with me through some very difficult times, and I know He can do the same for you.

Just this week I went through some rough spots. Rejection was not just tapping at my door; it was pounding like a SWAT team. A few things happened that shouldn't have happened. My feelings got hurt, and I had to decide: Am I going to bow to the way I feel and the lies swirling in my head, or am I going to live what I'm writing about in this book about rejection? I may hear other people's voices telling me one thing; my own thoughts may even be saying the same, but do those things line up with God's Word? These are the times when I must choose to keep the truth of who Jesus says I am above the level of all the other noise. And that is what I will choose over and over again.

Now, you may be asking, *Can it possibly be so easy? Can I just reject rejection—and it will never bother me again?* That would be nice, but the honest answer is no, of course not. If dealing with rejection was so simple, it wouldn't be much of a battle, would it? This is war, and the enemy is determined, so we must be even more relentless in resisting the enemy's lies and believing God's truth. There is evil, betrayal, and inhumanity in the world. People get hurt. But there is also hope, beauty, and promise. God is in the midst of us, His power and love are limitless, and the enemy loses in the end (Zephaniah 3:17 NKJV; 1 Chronicles 29:11; Revelation 20:10).

We are on a journey of learning and growing closer to Christ, and we have work to do along the way. We need to know the Word of God in order to silence the lies of the enemy—and allow the healing of God to flow and our confidence in Him to soar. This must become a part of who we are. And as with anything, as we do it more and more, it becomes easier and more natural. When we develop the art of rejecting the lies of rejection, the nights become more peaceful, and those racing thoughts quiet.

> *The Word of God silences the lies of the enemy.*

Know Your Enemy

The first step in winning any battle is understanding who you are fighting. We must identify our *true* enemy. When we are in pain, the blame game begins, and the people who have wronged us become the obvious targets. We can see nothing but them. After all, we need someone to blame. We blame the person who hurt us. We ask, "How *could* they?" We blame ourselves, asking, "What's wrong with me?" There may be lessons to be learned in those questions, but we don't need to camp out and stay there, because there is a real villain lying in wait to do even more damage: Satan. Unless we address his lies directly, he will simply find someone else to work through and continue his war against us.

Sun Tzu, a Chinese military general said, "If you know the enemy and know yourself, you need not fear the result of a hundred battles."[16] Overcoming rejection is a battle. Rejection is a tool the enemy of our soul, the devil, loves to use. He's the puppet master manipulating people's insecurities, carnal desires, and selfishness as tools to use against others. If he can keep us all hurting one another and then believing the lies those wounds open us to, then he can succeed in distracting us from the good plans God has for us. John 8:44 makes clear that Satan is an enemy who loves to lie to us:

> He was a murderer from the beginning, not holding to the truth, for there is no truth in him. When he lies, he speaks his native language, for he is a liar and the father of lies.

When we understand that what Satan says to us is nothing but lies and only lies, we can choose to reject them. In John 10:10, Jesus offers us great hope. He says, "The thief comes only to steal and kill and destroy; I have come that they may have life, and have it to the full."

Reject Rejection, Not People

When we say "reject rejection," we don't mean holding attitudes such as *You can't break up with me, because I'm breaking up with you* or *You can't fire me; I quit!* This is not that. This is not rejecting someone before they can reject you. Rather, it is refusing to allow rejection itself to have power over you. It is rejecting the rejection itself and standing on the truth instead.

At the same time, to reject rejection doesn't mean you should deny or hide from it. Give yourself time to feel. Acknowledge the hurt. Deal with it in a healthy way. Don't let it hold you, stop you, or keep you from choosing God's truth over the lies your adversary wants to shroud you in. This is about waging the *right* war.

Identifying your real enemy is quite freeing. You see, we have no control over what other people do. We can waste our time and energy trying, but we will never control their choices, and even God won't take away their free will. So rather than fighting the people who hurt you, fight against the lies that Satan is using against you. Yes, you have people to deal with and difficult decisions to make about relationships, and in the chapters to come we will dig into those things too. We cannot run from the hard things or avoid confrontation. There may be hope for a currently troubled relationship or it may be drawing to an end, but endlessly fighting with someone and harboring bitterness will only lead to more heartache. We fight against *rejection*—not the person who is rejecting us. We deal with them, but as we do, we remember that at times, they are simply tools the enemy is using against us.

Pick Up Your Weapons

There is a reason the Bible describes the Word of God as a sword (Ephesians 6:17; Hebrews 4:12): It cuts through the lies and separates deceit from truth. God gave the Word to us as a weapon both to protect ourselves and to use as we fight back against the enemy.

> The word of God is alive and active. Sharper than any double-edged sword, it penetrates even to dividing soul and spirit, joints and marrow; it judges the thoughts and attitudes of the heart.
>
> Hebrews 4:12

The enemy may fill our minds with lies about who God is, but the Bible reveals God's true character to us. When the enemy's lies lead us to feel bad about ourselves, we discover in God's Word who He created us to be. In its pages, we experience the unmerited, unconditional, never-ending love of Jesus, which defeats all rejection. God's Word is a powerful weapon, but we must pick it up and study it. It won't do any good sitting on a shelf. It must hold a prominent place in our hearts.

Good soldiers know their equipment well, and as believers, we are wise to know God's Word well and to understand how to use it. One of the best Scripture passages for this is Ephesians 6:11–18. It will help you to arm yourself from head to toe for the battle against rejection and other spiritual conflicts. This passage tells us to:

> Put on the whole armor of God, that you may be able to stand against the schemes of the devil. For we do not wrestle against flesh and blood, but against the rulers, against the authorities, against the cosmic powers over this present darkness, against the spiritual forces of evil in the heavenly places. Therefore take up the whole armor of God, that you may be able to withstand in the evil day, and having done all, to stand firm.
>
> Ephesians 6:11–13 ESV

> *Dress yourself in the armor of God.*

Would you rather be a warrior or live defeated? Get dressed in the "whole armor of God" and fight back! What are the pieces of this armor?

- The belt of truth (v. 14)
- The breastplate of righteousness (v. 14)
- The shoes of peace (v. 15)
- The shield of faith (v. 16)
- The helmet of salvation (v. 17)
- "The sword of the Spirit, *which is the word of God*" (v. 17, emphasis mine)

Once you're in your armor and wielding your sword and shield, don't enter into battle just yet. There is yet another weapon that God has given us—prayer. Ephesians 6:18 says:

> And pray in the Spirit on all occasions with all kinds of prayers and requests. With this in mind, be alert and always keep on praying for all the Lord's people.

Prayer focuses our attention on the source of our strength and invites Him in. Simply ask, and God will go before you. He is your rear guard (Isaiah 52:12). In other words, He's got your back. The Bible tells us more than once that the battle belongs to the Lord (1 Samuel 17:47; 2 Chronicles 20:15). If you go up against the devil in your own strength, you're fighting a losing battle already. But, through prayer, submit yourself to God, and the enemy will run.

> Submit yourselves therefore to God. Resist the devil, and he will flee from you.
>
> James 4:7 ESV

I love the way the Message translation renders this verse. It makes me feel feisty.

> So let God work his will in you. Yell a loud *no* to the Devil and watch him make himself scarce. Say a quiet *yes* to God and he'll be there in no time.
>
> James 4:7 MSG

And here is fantastic news: The Bible says that you are guaranteed victory. With God on your side, you can't lose!

> Little children, you are from God and have overcome them, for he who is in you is greater than he who is in the world.
>
> 1 John 4:4 ESV

Truth versus Lies

Let's dig in and attack rejection's lies one by one. When the enemy whispers a lie to you, reject it with God's truth. Here are some examples.

Lie:

"They left me. Therefore, I'm unworthy of love."

Truth:

"I am precious to God; He loves me and will never leave me."

God's Word:

How precious to me are your thoughts, God! How vast is the sum of them! Were I to count them, they would outnumber the grains of sand—when I awake, I am still with you.

Psalm 139:17–18

Lie:

"Maybe I'm not meant to be happy."

Truth:

"God promises good things ahead for me."

God's Word:

For His anger is but for a moment, His favor is for a lifetime. Weeping may endure for a night, but a shout of joy comes in the morning.

Psalm 30:5 AMP

Lie:

"They betrayed me. Now I can't trust anyone."

Truth:

"God does not lie. I can trust Him."

God's Word:

God is not human, that he should lie, not a human being, that he should change his mind. Does he speak and then not act? Does he promise and not fulfill?

Numbers 23:19

Lie:

"They hurt me, and God doesn't care."

Truth:

"God takes it personally when people mistreat me, and He is working on my behalf."

God's Word:

For whoever touches you touches the apple of his eye.

Zechariah 2:8

I like the way the International Children's Bible renders this verse: "Whoever hurts you hurts what is precious to me" (Zechariah 2:8 ICB).

Lie:

"I can't risk loving other people; I'll just get hurt again."

Truth:

"God enables me to love without fear."

God's Word:

There is no fear in love. But perfect love drives out fear.

1 John 4:18

These are merely some of the lies of rejection and the truths that counter them. There are countless more. Joyce and I encourage you to create your own list. Keep it close. Post it where you can see it, and combat the lies you may have believed with truth from Scripture. Get feisty. Shout to the enemy: "No! I'm not falling for your tricks. And the God who lives in me is far greater than you!"

As I get older, I realize even more how vital this is. You don't outgrow the opportunity to be rejected. Rejection still hurts, and those wounds can build a tough armor of scar tissue, hardening your heart and changing your view of who God says you are—unless you deal with them quickly, one by one. Let the healing do its job as early as possible, and put on God's armor to combat rejection's lies instead of building up your own armor, which doesn't work anyway.

Stay Alert

Remember, as Joyce says, the enemy's favorite battleground is our mind. We must guard it diligently. When our thoughts are swirling and we feel ourselves believing something negative, it most likely does not line up with God's Word. See what the Bible says. Get out your sword and begin swinging.

> Do not conform to the pattern of this world, but be transformed by the renewing of your mind. Then you will be able to test and approve what God's will is—his good, pleasing and perfect will.
>
> Romans 12:2

Lean in Closer

1. What are some examples of lies that rejection has whispered to you?
   - That you're unloved, unwanted, or unworthy
   _____
   _____

   - That no one cares
   _____
   _____

   - That it's all your fault—you deserve to be rejected
   _____
   _____

   - That you'll never truly be accepted
   _____
   _____

2. What are your thoughts on beginning to reject rejection, and how might you put them into action?
   _____
   _____

3. What does John 8:44 tell you about who your true enemy is? How does this affect you and your outlook on the people who have hurt you?
   _____
   _____

4. Be careful not to deny your pain. Instead, refuse to allow rejection itself to have such power over you by relentlessly holding on to the truth of God's Word. How can you acknowledge the hurt now, release it to God, and begin waging the *right* war?
   _____
   _____

5. How does John 10:10 bring you hope?
   _____
   _____

6. Beginning with the examples of lies and truth in this chapter, create your personal battle plan by writing any lies the enemy has told you and the truth from God's Word to dispel each one.
   _____
   _____

CHAPTER 12

Accepting Yourself

Joyce

So we have come to know and to believe the love that God has for us. God is love, and whoever abides in love abides in God, and God abides in him.

1 John 4:16 ESV

We spend more time with ourselves than with anyone else, so just think about how miserable we will be if we reject ourselves. I rejected myself until I was in my forties. I constantly found fault with myself and would have preferred to be anyone but me. As I mentioned earlier, I tried to be like so many people that I didn't know who I was. I tried to be like others because I didn't like myself. I was rejecting myself. When some people experience rejection, they automatically assume that being rejected means something is wrong with them. They then begin to reject themselves and become people-pleasers, hoping that if they become what everyone else wants them to be, they will be accepted and can then accept themselves.

I had to learn to accept God's love for me and learn to love myself. To love yourself is simply to receive the love God offers you. I urge you to accept and embrace yourself just as you are, because God loves and accepts you. You may need to grow in some areas, but God will work with you and take care of the areas that need improvement as you mature spiritually in Him.

One of the wonderful lessons I have learned in life is that I can enjoy myself while God is changing me. Thankfully, I don't have to wait until I'm perfect to enjoy myself and my life—and neither do you. Why don't you take the pressure off yourself and come to peace terms with yourself. I once read an amusing motto, "It is time to make peace with your thighs." ☺ What the author meant, I think, is that we need to accept ourselves and enjoy life despite our imperfections or things we wish were different about ourselves. Think about what you don't like about yourself and, one by one, accept those things as they are. Then, if any changes are needed, trust God to make them.

> *Enjoy yourself while God changes you.*

If you reject yourself, you will probably reject others. We can give others only what we have in ourselves. I can't love you if I don't love me; I can't accept you as you are if I don't accept myself as I am. When I say you should accept yourself as you are, you may immediately think of all the things you still do wrong, but God knows about all those things, and He loves you anyway. If your desire is to change and be as God wants you to be, He is pleased with you. His love for you is unconditional, and it is His love that heals people.

Truly, Wholly, Completely Accepted

The key to accepting yourself is to believe that God accepts you completely and unconditionally. If rejection is the withdrawal of love, then unconditional love is the antidote for it. And it is available from one source only. Ephesians 1:6 tells us we are "accepted in the beloved" (KJV). What does this mean? "The beloved" refers to Jesus, and His sacrifice makes each one of us acceptable—including our flaws, mistakes, and wounds. He makes *you* acceptable.

Jesus redeemed us from the pain of this world by taking it upon Himself, something He chose to do, despite its great cost. He graciously opened His arms and accepted us permanently, and when His work on the cross was complete, He said, "It is finished" (John 19:30). It is finished! Your acceptance is binding and permanent and forever, never to be revoked. Father God is so pleased with His Son, Jesus, who gave His all for us, that by His grace and through our faith, He lovingly welcomes us into His arms. We are never rejected, and always accepted.

It isn't easy to work through the past, to feel the pain, or to risk hoping again. But the alternative to dwelling in those painful places is receiving the beautiful promises of God. You may have been hurt, and some things may never be the same even after you experience God's healing. Your life may look different in some ways, but you will have something you may never have had otherwise. You will undoubtedly know in your heart that you are loved by God—truly, wholly, completely, and perfectly loved. Yes, at times, people do hurtful things, but they can never take away what God has given you.

Be Amazed

You will be absolutely amazed at how your life will change and how much peace and joy you will have if you accept yourself instead of rejecting yourself. You can learn to be your own best friend. When I didn't like myself, I wanted to be doing something all the time because busyness distracted me from the feelings of rejection that plagued me. Now I love to be with myself, and I enjoy time alone. Even if you don't like something about yourself, don't let it stop you from loving yourself. I have a friend who is quite a bit overweight, but she is secure and confident. Yes, she would love to be smaller, but losing weight is a challenge for her, and she refuses to let it control her life and make her unhappy with who she is. You are more than what you look like.

> *You are an amazing person.*

You are an amazing person. A masterpiece, one of a kind, and that makes you precious.

> We are God's masterpiece. He has created us anew in Christ Jesus, so we can do the good things he planned for us long ago.
>
> Ephesians 2:10 NLT

God says: "You are precious and honored in my sight" (Isaiah 43:4). Each life is truly a gift from God, and we can honor His gift by cherishing our own life as well as respecting the value of others. You can stay amazed if you take time to think about how your human body is put together and what is required to keep it running properly every day. Consider these facts:

- Your heart beats about 100,000 times a day.[17]
- Every second your body makes 2 million new red blood cells.[18]
- Approximately 330 billion cells are replaced in your body every day.[19]
- Your body contains about six quarts of blood, and it circulates through your body three times every minute. In one day, it travels 12,000 miles, which is four times across the United States from coast to coast.[20]

See? Your body is truly amazing, and *you are truly amazing*. Begin to see yourself the way God sees you, and you will be astounded.

Be Courageous

It requires courage to be who you truly are instead of becoming a people-pleaser—one who tries to keep everyone else happy while sacrificing your personal happiness. We are all different and have a God-given privilege to be ourselves. For years, I thought I was weird, but now I know I am unique. Being called by God to teach His Word required that I focus on that calling rather than spending a lot of time doing ordinary things other women did. Often, the devil put in my head the thought that I wasn't a regular woman or a normal woman. But who determines what is normal?

I spent about a year at one point trying to be what I thought was "normal." I tried to learn how to sew so I could make some of my family's clothes. I bought a sewing machine and took sewing lessons. I made Dave a pair of shorts and a shirt, but when I finished the shorts, the pockets were longer than the shorts, and I hemmed the shirt sleeves up on the outside instead of under on the inside.

I hated sewing but kept trying to do it because a friend of mine sewed. She also had a garden, so I tried to have one, too. We lived next door to one another, and one night some bugs attacked my garden and left big holes in my tomatoes. But the bugs didn't touch her tomatoes. I asked God why He didn't protect my tomatoes, because I had prayed over my garden, and He whispered in my heart that He never told me to grow tomatoes, so He had no obligation to protect them.

There are times we fail at things simply because they aren't what God wants us to do. God had called me to teach His Word, not to sew and tend a garden. But He had to let me try and fail so He could teach me to be myself. There are times when other people try to talk us into doing what they are doing. But if we don't believe we should do those things, we need to respectfully stand our ground and not do them just because we want to please someone.

I tried several different things in an effort to be "normal," and they all failed—and made me miserable. Eventually I learned the lesson I am sharing with you, which is that you must be yourself and like who you are. If you don't follow your own heart, you will not be able to respect yourself. Don't waste your time thinking over and over about everything that is wrong with you. If God convicts you of something that needs to change, then work with the Holy Spirit to make the change. Otherwise, just enjoy who you are in Christ.

> Be yourself and like who you are.

When God called Joshua to take over for Moses after Moses died, He didn't say, "Go and be like Moses." He said, "As I was with Moses, so I will be with you" (Joshua 1:5). It is not important for us to be like someone else; it is only important that God is with us, and He can enable us to do whatever His will is for us.

The apostle Paul said that if he had tried to please people instead of pleasing God, he would not have been a "servant of Christ" (Galatians 1:10). This is a sobering thought. We can miss God's will for our lives if we are focused on trying to be popular and accepted by everyone instead of seeking what He wants for us. When I obeyed God's call to ministry, lost my friends, and was asked to leave my church, I would have missed God's will for my life if acceptance had been more important to me than obedience to God. It saddens me to think of how many people are miserable because they don't like and accept themselves.

We need to learn to love others as God loves us. We need to love people for who they are, not who we want them to be. When we accept people, they are often inspired to want to change and be better. But when we reject them, they are more likely to resist change. Take it from one who knows very well: You

> *Love people for who they are, not who we want them to be.*

cannot change people; only God can do that. In addition, you cannot make other people love or accept themselves. But you can pray for them, trusting God to work in their hearts and minds as only He can.

Say No When Necessary

No is a small yet powerful word, one many of us need to say more often. In society today, many people are extremely stressed because they are trying to do everything other people want them to do. The problem with this is everyone seems to want us to do something different. We are not responsible for meeting everyone's expectations. We are responsible for following the guidance of the Holy Spirit for our life.

We all want to be accepted and well thought of. We want people to like us and be pleased with us, and for that to happen we think we have to say yes even when our heart screams no. A courageous person will follow their heart and be true to themselves and to God. If I say yes to doing things and then find myself complaining about them, it is a good sign I am doing something I should not have done. We are to follow peace, not people.

> *Follow peace, not people.*

If you are stressed and want to have more peace, simply write on a piece of paper all the things you are committed to doing. Then go over each entry on the list and, one by one, ask yourself why you are doing it. Unless your motive is to obey God or because you feel it is the right thing to do, you should cross it off your list. If you are doing it because someone expects you to do it, then you are doing it for the wrong reason.

Let me say that there are times when we should do something we may not want to do for someone, but in those times, we will know it is the right thing to do even though we would rather not do it. Someone recently asked me to do something that would take about three hours of my time. Even though I would have liked to decline, I knew I needed to do it because the person who asked me to do it has done several things for me when I asked them to. We don't have to want to do everything we do, but we should do it with a good attitude and be at peace as we do it.

Sacrifice for the Right Reasons

Being unselfish and willing to sacrifice is part of our walk with God; however, God desires obedience more than sacrifice (1 Samuel 15:22). If we are sacrificing in obedience to God, then it is a good thing, but if we are doing it to keep people happy while knowing it is not what God wants us to do, then it is a problem that causes loss of joy and peace.

How many things do you do simply to keep someone from getting angry with you? I grew up being afraid of my father's anger, and I did everything I could do to keep him from getting angry. When he did become angry, I became the peacemaker in the house and did everything I could to restore peace. I carried my fear of angry people into my adult life, and although I am much, much better, I still must resist the temptation to give in to someone just because I know they get angry easily, and I don't want to deal with the anger. This is especially true when I am dealing with someone in my family or with a close friend. If you are living under the fear of rejection, you may behave the same way.

Be Free

Being healed or made whole doesn't mean you are never tempted to revert to old ways. Many things are not a temptation for me at all now, but some things that remind me of my father require me to resist the temptation to fall back into old patterns. I think it is important for you to know this because I don't want you to feel that you are not healed just because you still must resist some temptations. Before God healed me, I simply reacted in old ways without even realizing I was doing it. But now I recognize what the devil is trying to do, and I don't react; I act according to the leading of the Holy Spirit. At least I do so most of the time. Occasionally, I fall into the old trap again, but it doesn't take me long to get out of it.

Jesus died for you to be free from sin and death (Romans 8:2), but also free to live the life you were meant to live (Galatians 5:1). No matter how far away you currently are from the life God has in mind for you, you can learn to accept and even embrace yourself. *You can be healed.*

"He himself bore our sins" in his body on the cross, so that we might die to sins and live for righteousness; "by his wounds you have been healed."

1 Peter 2:24

Lean in Closer

1. First John 4:16 says, "So we have come to know and to believe the love that God has for us" (ESV). How does this verse comfort you?

   _____
   _____

2. In what ways do you feel you reject yourself? Why is it important to learn to accept yourself instead?

   _____
   _____

3. How does this statement encourage you: "Yes, at times, people do hurtful things, but they can never take away what God has given you"?

   _____
   _____

4. Joyce states that we can only give to others what we have in ourselves. She writes, "I can't love you if I don't love me; I can't accept you as you are if I don't accept myself as I am." What does this say about the importance of loving and accepting yourself?

   _____
   _____

5. Are you a people-pleaser? Think about the things you do or have done simply to keep someone else from being unhappy or angry at you.

   _____

Accepting Yourself

6. Think about all the things on your to-do list. Which ones did you say yes to when you wanted to say no? Pray and ask God to help you grow in courage and to do only the things you can do for the right reasons.

7. You are free to live the life you were meant to live and to become who God made you to be. Make a list of the things you like about yourself, even the small things. Be generous with this list, and begin discovering the path toward courageously liking and accepting yourself.

CHAPTER 13

Your Past Is Not Your Future

Ginger

You've gone into my future to prepare the way, and in kindness you follow behind me to spare me from the harm of my past.

Psalm 139:5 TPT

There comes a time when we must purposefully step out of the darkness of the way things have been and envision a bright future—one of hope, healing, and confidence. When your life has been shaped by rejection, it can be difficult to see that it could be any other way. You may have not only experienced years of pain but also built an entire lifestyle around trying to avoid more. But those days are past. This is a new day.

Do phrases such as these play repeatedly in your head?

- *They hurt me so badly.*
- *Nothing ever changes.*
- *It's too late.*
- *I'm not that strong.*

You may have resigned yourself to the idea that you'll always bleed just a little bit. But let me assure you, you are not beyond repair. Our God is so much bigger than anything you've been through. If He can heal others and fill them with hope and a sense of purpose—and He *has*—He can do the same for you.

Joyce felt completely alone and thought that she was the only one enduring such horrific sexual abuse. She was afraid she would never experience joy in her life, but God has brought her joy in abundance and used her story to help countless others. I didn't know how to turn off the images of my husband's betrayal that plagued my mind, and I didn't think I could ever trust again after his rejection, but God helped me to do both, and I am free. What He has done for Joyce and me—and so many others—we believe He will also do for you.

Faith is powerful. Ask God to help you believe in a bright future, a future in which rejection doesn't permeate your thoughts and direct your actions. Envision a life of wholeness, healthy connection with people, and true freedom. Rely on God as you choose to hold on to faith when you have yet to see the evidence; it will come. Standing on faith in God also means no longer striving to do in your own power what needs to be done in your life. This is a reminder I need often because I love to attempt to fix my own problems. When you don't know how to change or what to do differently, God's Holy Spirit is right there to help, praying for you and guiding you every step of the way.

> Likewise the Spirit helps us in our weakness. For we do not know what to pray for as we ought, but the Spirit himself intercedes for us with groanings too deep for words. And he who searches hearts knows what is the mind of the Spirit, because the Spirit intercedes for the saints according to the will of God. And we know that for those who love God all things work together for good, for those who are called according to his purpose.
> Romans 8:26–28 ESV

God promises good for you, and no person can thwart the plans He has for your life. Romans 8:31 says, "What then shall we say to these things? If God is for us, who can be against us?" (ESV). God is for you. He believes in you and is your strongest ally. Nothing that comes against you stands a chance.

Biblical Examples of Rejection

There are many examples in Scripture of people who were violently rejected, yet God restored and used them in mighty ways. King David comes to my mind first. He faced massive rejection. He was the boy whose own father didn't even think he was worthy of being introduced to the prophet Samuel, who was searching for a potential king (1 Samuel 16:10–13). He was the only one of eight sons not to be presented. That must have felt like a slap in David's face. David was also rejected by King Saul—the man he had served wholeheartedly. Not only did Saul try to kill David, but he hunted him down to be murdered (1 Samuel 19:1–18; 23:7–24:22). Yet God handpicked David above all others.

David loved and served God, but this didn't stop him from being rejected. Some of his own men turned against him at one point (1 Samuel 30:6). David's wife mocked and despised him (2 Samuel 6:16–22). His own son Absalom tried to overthrow his kingdom (2 Samuel 15:1–18:16). It was all so painful that he wrote often about rejection in his psalms.

> All my enemies whisper together against me; they imagine the worst for me... Even my close friend, someone I trusted, one who shared my bread, has turned against me.
>
> Psalm 41:7, 9

Tell God what you feel.

In this psalm, David cries out to God: "This hurts!" You, too, can openly share your pain and confusion with Him. You can safely tell God what you feel, that what you are going through is agony, and that you don't understand. Despite David's pain, he always comes back around to God's faithfulness.

> When the righteous cry for help, the Lord hears and delivers them out of all their troubles. The Lord is near to the brokenhearted and saves the crushed in spirit. Many are the afflictions of the righteous, but the Lord delivers him out of them all.
>
> Psalm 34:17–19 ESV

Moses was a leader of many, and he reminds us that leadership is hard. He was rejected by the very people he fought for time after time (Numbers 16). When they were in danger, they rejected his direction (Numbers 14:41–45). When they were hungry, they blamed him (Exodus 16:2–3). When they were tired of the same food, they turned on him (Numbers 11:4–6). Moses didn't like it, and he became troubled and upset by their complaining (Numbers 11:10–15). But he remained faithful to his calling and led them to the door of the Promised Land (Deuteronomy 34:1–4). God honored him in Hebrews 11, which is considered the Bible's faith hall of fame (vv. 23–28).

Let's think also about another Old Testament leader, Samuel. Samuel, the prophet who anointed David to be king, was rejected by the elders of Israel who demanded a human king when God was right there to lead them personally (1 Samuel 8:4–6). In 1 Samuel 8:7–8 (ESV), the Lord tells Samuel:

> Obey the voice of the people in all that they say to you, for they have not rejected you, but they have rejected me from being king over them. According to all the deeds that they have done, from the day I brought them up out of Egypt even to this day, forsaking me and serving other gods, so they are also doing to you.

This scripture is reassuring as well as eye-opening, because it tells us that rejection may be about more than we see on the surface. I wonder how many times we are rejected because we are following what we believe God is asking of us and others disagree or don't like it.

David, Moses, and Samuel remind us that leadership can be lonely. Not everyone will like our decisions. We may face rejection, but what we do is vital. You see, God doesn't guarantee that we won't experience rejection. But He does understand and care about our pain, and He is faithful to help us through our challenges, especially when our heart's desire is to serve Him as well as the people we lead.

One of my favorite examples of rejection in the Bible is the woman Jesus met at the well. We read her story in John 4:3–42. She was a rejected woman from a rejected people, the Samaritans, with whom the Jews did not associate. Neither her heritage nor the sin in her life kept Jesus from her. She was the very first person to whom Jesus revealed himself as the Messiah. Wow! An unclean, shunned woman. Jesus looked at her and knew all, yet He also saw her as worthy of restoring, redeeming, and embracing. She took His message to many, and they believed (John 4:39).

The woman with the issue of blood in Luke 8:43–48 was rejected by people because of her illness and the way Jewish law viewed her condition as unclean. They would have nothing to do with her, yet she touched Jesus, just brushed the hem of his clothing, and was healed. Jesus heals the rejected.

Look up the stories I have mentioned for yourself. Read them and build your faith. There are many more stories to discover. God is the champion of the brokenhearted.

> *God is the champion of the brokenhearted.*

Famously Overlooked

Many people we would undoubtedly call successful also faced rejection, but it didn't stop them.

- Abraham Lincoln lost jobs, elections, and faced many personal hardships.[21]
- In 1919, Walt Disney was fired and his editor told him he "lacked imagination and had no original ideas."[22]
- Before her wildly successful show, *I Love Lucy*, Lucille Ball's drama instructors urged her to try another profession.[23]

- During her lifetime, and while writing nearly 1,800 pieces of work, fewer than a dozen of Emily Dickinson's poems were accepted for publication in her lifetime.[24]
- In his first role, actor Harrison Ford, was told by the head of new talent, "You're never going to make it in the business. Just forget about it." Thankfully, he didn't, and his performances as Han Solo and Indiana Jones live on.[25]

Rejection May Serve a Purpose

When you experience rejection, I encourage you to ask yourself, *Where might this rejection take me?* Walt Disney said, "All the adversity I've had in my life, all my troubles and obstacles, have strengthened me... You may not realize it when it happens, but a kick in the teeth may be the best thing in the world for you."[26] Even painful rejection can be motivating, but more than that, I like to consider what miracles God can bring about through it.

> *Ask yourself where rejection might take you.*

In Genesis 45:8, Joseph tells his brothers, who sold him into slavery, "It was not you who sent me here, but God. He made me father to Pharaoh, lord of his entire household and ruler of all Egypt." Joseph says later to his brothers, "You intended to harm me, but God intended it for good to accomplish what is now being done, the saving of many lives" (Genesis 50:20). Through their terrible act, God took Joseph to a place of honor and saved many people from starvation. This reminds us not to give either the person who rejects us or the devil too much credit. That's more power than they deserve. God is the one who holds power over all. Deuteronomy 7:21 says, "Do not be terrified by them, for the Lord your God, who is among you, is a great and awesome God." Just reading this brings peace to my soul and a smile to my face.

Rejection is always a possibility. But without risk, our lives are without growth, real relationships, or progress. I often pray that God would hide me from evil. I ask that He shelter me under the shadow of His wing and take me where He wants me, when He wants me. So, could it be that God is using even rejection as a means to do that? Could it be a form of protection or an answer to prayer? Could it be that heartbreak is not what God intended for you, but can He use it all for good in your life? Absolutely! Reject the lies of rejection, but embrace the lessons to be learned through it. Listen with an open heart for changes that need to be made in your life. Begin thinking differently. Begin to believe and say "God will use this for my good."

> *Embrace the lessons learned through rejection.*

It's beautiful redemption and sweet revenge for good to come out of what the enemy meant for evil. God may use an experience with rejection to redirect you, open new doors, and take you down paths you might otherwise miss. He may use it to protect you from relationships that aren't best for you or from other bad situations and people in the future. Through it, He can give you more empathy, love, and compassion for others who have experienced similar situations.

Your past is not your future. Your pain is not wasted. You're learning to see things differently, think differently, and trust in a faithful God for more than you ever imagined possible.

Lean in Closer

1. What does Romans 8:26–28 ESV say to you about your future being brighter than your past?

   _____

   _____

2. David writes openly in Psalms about his rejection and pain. Which verses about this heartache can you relate to? Which verses inspire you to trust God more?

   _____
   _____

3. In what ways do you relate to these biblical stories of rejection and healing?
   - David

   _____
   _____

   - Moses

   _____
   _____

   - Samuel

   _____
   _____

   - The woman at the well

   _____
   _____

   - The woman with the issue of blood

   _____
   _____

4. In what ways have people overlooked you, dismissed you, or tried to put limits on your potential? What does God's Word say about you that disputes their words and actions?

   _____
   _____

5. Identify ways God has taken your rejection experience and used it for your good, or may do so in the future. Check all that apply and add others that come to mind:
   - To develop empathy and compassion
   - To protect you from unhealthy relationships

- To open new doors and take you where He wants you
- To spare you from more pain down the road
- Others: _____
  _____

CHAPTER 14

Hurting People Hurt People

Joyce

Be merciful, just as your Father is merciful.

Luke 6:36

Learning the lessons I will share with you in this chapter was a huge key toward my healing. I believe one reason God is merciful to us is that He knows why we do the things we do. He doesn't simply look at *what* we did but also at *why* we did it. When I behaved badly years ago, God knew the pain I had gone through, and He was merciful and patient in dealing with me. At times, when people asked me, "Why do you act like that?" I had to ask myself, "Act like what?" I didn't know what I was doing or why I was doing it. One of the lessons God taught me is that *hurting people hurt people*. This helped me greatly when I realized I needed to forgive my father.

I don't know all the details of how my father was raised. Based on what I have heard, I know his father, my grandfather, was ill-tempered. I am certain that my father was treated badly and suffered while growing up. And I strongly believe that incest was in his family. There is no doubt my father was a "hurting person," and that is why he caused so much pain for other people.

I have encountered many wounded people in my life and ministry, and very often those people do hurt other people. They act out of their own pain. Studies show that one-third of children who are abused grow up to become abusers.[27] An abuser can leave a legacy of abuse, but the first person in an abused family who receives Jesus as their Lord and Savior can put a stop to the generational curse of abuse. I believe

> *Receive Jesus as your Lord and Savior.*

this happened in my life and family, and I believe the same can happen to anyone else if they will apply God's Word to their life. We don't have to inherit bad things from our relatives, because we are co-heirs with Jesus, and we inherit everything He has received from His Father (Romans 8:17). When you receive Jesus, you become part of God's family, and you receive the same rights and privileges that Jesus has by faith.

Through counseling, Ginger and Tim uncovered pain and fear in Tim's life that played a role in his addiction. Because he was exposed to pornography at around eight years old, his innocence was stolen. This caused a deep wound.

When you are hurt by someone, it helps to realize they may be acting out of their own hurt. It doesn't negate what happened, and it is certainly not an excuse to inflict pain on other people. But understanding that people hurt others for a reason—which is that they have been hurt themselves—gives us a perspective that aids in our healing.

Sarah's Story Continues

Remember our friend Sarah who shared her story in chapter 4? Understanding God's unconditional acceptance and that hurting people hurt people made a big difference when she recently met her birth mother. Here is how she describes it:

> I had the opportunity to practice this dawning wisdom [that hurting people hurt people] just last month when I met my birth mother for the first time. For much of my life, I thought understanding my origin story would fill in the missing puzzle piece of who I am. And I thought meeting my birth mother and finally experiencing her love firsthand might finally allow me to heal from the fear of rejection and abandonment that has followed me throughout my life. But because of what I have begun to learn, I was able to go to that meeting filled not with a sense of need and the accompanying terror of being

> rejected yet again. Instead, I was filled with a sense of gratitude and compassion—for my birth mother and the terrible rejection and abandonment that she had experienced when she became pregnant with me; for my amazing parents, who have shown me the closest thing I've ever known in human terms to the love of Christ; and finally, for the person I am and have become, through all of the pain and struggle and all of the joys of this life.

Do Yourself a Favor and Forgive

I want to tell you about the power of forgiveness, but first let me say that I know rejection hurts. The pain is real, and even though you forgive, it doesn't mean the pain will immediately go away. I know a man whose wife just told him she wants a divorce, and he was shocked. They have been married for close to twenty years, and although they had difficulties, partially due to sexual abuse in her childhood, they were working on their marriage. He feels deeply rejected, and when I called him recently to see how he was doing, he said some days are not so bad and others are horrible.

While you are healing from rejection, you will experience a wide range of emotions, and some days will be better than others. The more you keep your mind off the event that hurt you, the better your days will be; however, you can't help but think about it at times, and it will hurt. I recommend embracing the pain—instead of fighting it—when it comes. The pain is part of the healing process, and the more you fight it, the longer the healing will take.

Pain is part of the healing process.

I like to use the example of a badly skinned knee. I once fell and ripped the skin off my knee. It hurt when it happened, but it hurt worse when a scab began to form. But the scab was necessary to protect the wound while it was healing from the inside out.

Scabs often form over emotional wounds, figuratively speaking, just as physical scabs form over physical wounds. A person picks the scab off of emotional wounds, so to speak, by continually thinking and talking about them. If you keep picking the scab off your emotional wounds, you will end up with scars that may never go away. There is a time to talk about and express your pain, but there is also a time to let it go; otherwise, you will never heal. You can't go back and change your past, but you can do what is needed to have a great future. I often say, "I didn't have a good start in life, but I am determined to have a great finish."

It seems unjust to be asked to forgive someone who has deeply wounded you. The person who hurt you may not deserve your forgiveness, but you deserve peace, and you will never have it without forgiveness. As Ginger mentioned in chapter 6, before you can forgive, you must know that forgiveness is not a feeling; it's a decision you make about how you will treat the person who hurt, rejected, or offended you.

Jesus made clear in His Word that forgiving our enemies is something we are expected to do as believers. We are to forgive others just as our heavenly Father forgives us. Jesus paid a high price for us to have our sins forgiven. He paid this price even though we didn't deserve for Him to do it. If we want to be like our Father in heaven, then we must forgive others their sins against us.

> Be kind and compassionate to one another, forgiving each other, just as in Christ God forgave you.
>
> Ephesians 4:32

Not only must we forgive, but we also need to bless those who hurt or wrong us.

> But to you who are listening I say: Love your enemies, do good to those who hate you, bless those who curse you, pray for those who mistreat you.
>
> Luke 6:27–28

As Ginger mentioned in chapter 11, the devil often hurts us by working through people. Because this is true, it's also true that we allow him to keep hurting us if we refuse to forgive people who hurt us. The best way to get the devil back for hurting you is to do good to those who hurt you. Jesus says we are to love our enemies, pray for them to be blessed, and help them if they are in need (Matthew 5:44; 25:35–40; Luke 6:27–36). Paul quotes Him in Romans 12:20: "If your enemy is hungry, feed him; if he is thirsty, give him something to drink. In doing this, you will heap burning coals on his head." When you begin to pray for someone who hurt you, your feelings toward them will improve. Also, helping them if they have a need is powerful. It will help them with whatever they need, and it will help you heal.

I never had loving *feelings* toward my parents, but I did love them because I chose to obey Romans 12:20. I prayed for them, and Dave and I took care of them for about fifteen years when they became elderly and couldn't take care of themselves physically or financially. I knew this was the right thing to do, and I did it with help from my daughters. I didn't necessarily feel love toward my parents, but love is not just a feeling; it is much more than that. My parents were in an assisted living nursing facility, and we paid the bill, got their groceries, did their laundry, took them to doctors' appointments, bought their clothes, and more.

> *Do what is right even when it feels wrong.*

Helping them in these ways was rarely convenient. When you do what is right when it feels wrong, you are growing spiritually.

Forgiveness and Prayer

We all want our prayers to be answered, but they won't be if we have unforgiveness in our hearts.

> Therefore, I tell you, whatever you ask for in prayer, believe that you have received it, and it will be yours. And when you stand praying, if you hold anything against anyone, forgive them, so that your Father in heaven may forgive you your sins.
>
> Mark 11:24–26

Multitudes of people have prayed a prayer of forgiveness for someone, but when they didn't feel any differently toward them, they thought they hadn't forgiven. So, it is important to know that forgiveness is not a feeling; it is a decision. And as I've pointed out, love is not a feeling, either. Both forgiveness and love can *produce* feelings, but what counts more than having feelings is that we make the decisions to forgive and to love and that we take the actions of forgiveness and love.

Before we pray, it is good to search our hearts to make sure we are not angry with anyone. The apostle Paul in his letter to the Ephesians says we should not let the sun go down on our anger, or we will give the devil a foothold in our life (Ephesians 4:26–27). Paul also instructs the Corinthians to forgive so Satan would not gain an advantage over them (2 Corinthians 2:10–11).

As difficult as it may be to extend forgiveness to someone, and as much as you may think they deserve *not* to be forgiven, if you pay attention to these scriptures, you can see that holding unforgiveness in your heart toward anyone is dangerous.

When you have been hurt, forgiving the person or people who hurt you is part of your own healing. Until you forgive, what they did to you will continue to gnaw at you. If you're not careful, you can become bitter, and that will make your condition worse.

> Get rid of all bitterness, rage and anger, brawling and slander, along with every form of malice. Be kind and compassionate to one another, forgiving each other, just as in Christ God forgave you.
>
> Ephesians 4:31–32

I have learned that the quicker I forgive, the easier it is to do. If I wait too long, unforgiveness will start to take root in my heart and be much more difficult to deal with later.

Unforgiveness Adds Stress

Holding on to unforgiveness adds stress to your life. Stress is behind many diseases, and it can become a dangerous health problem if not taken care of. Most people today would say they have too much stress in their life, and part of this, I believe, is simply because the world is a noisy, stressful place. Add to that a lifestyle that is too busy, then pile on anger and unforgiveness, and you have the makings of a very unhappy life—one that will eventually either explode or implode. I truly believe that when we forgive, we do ourselves a favor. The person I am angry with may not even know or care that I am angry with them, but holding on to unforgiveness eats away at my peace.

I think back on times when I could stay angry with Dave for two or three weeks. Now, I realize how ridiculous my behavior was, but then, I was controlled by my emotions. One day, Dave said, "Wouldn't it be a shame if Jesus came today, and you had spent your last day on earth angry?" This is a good question for all of us to think about.

I believe forgiveness is the beginning of all the healing our souls need. We need to receive God's forgiveness and forgive anyone we have anything against if we truly want to be healed.

> *Forgiveness is the beginning of healing.*

Lean in Closer

1. How does the fact that people who are hurting often end up hurting those around them impact you? How could this perspective open a door of forgiveness and healing in your life?

2. Joyce states, "I recommend embracing the pain—instead of fighting it—when it comes. The pain is part of the healing process, and the more you fight it, the longer the healing will take." Does this ring true for you? How will you embrace your pain and open your heart to God's healing?

3. Why are you doing yourself a favor when you forgive?

4. What can you learn about the power of forgiveness from Ephesians 4:31–32?

5. Have you ever thought about the fact that unforgiveness adds stress to a person's life? How have you experienced this personally or seen it in someone else's life?

6. Pray and ask God to reveal to you anyone you need to forgive. Because forgiveness is a choice rather than a feeling, write down your decisions so you can stand on them when your feelings tell you to do otherwise.

   _____

   _____

PART 4

Goodbye, Insecurity; Hello, Peace

For God gave us a spirit not of fear but of power and love and self-control.

2 Timothy 1:7 ESV

CHAPTER 15

Nurturing Confidence

Ginger

Blessed is the one who trusts in the Lord, whose confidence is in him.

Jeremiah 17:7

Rejection can throw a bucket of cold water on the fires of confidence, but confidence can still be yours. It is a gift from God, and it's yours for the unwrapping. It does not hinge on your talent, intelligence, or appearance. It isn't about what you do, how much money you have, or whether others embrace you. This confidence—the confidence that comes from *Him*—revolves around perfect love that casts out fear (1 John 4:18) and is freely given to all. It is important to realize that you can accept this gift, but you must also learn to put it to use.

I like the way Joyce describes confidence in her book *The Confident Woman*:

> A person without confidence is like an airplane sitting on a runway with empty fuel tanks. The plane has the ability to fly, but without some fuel, it's not getting off the ground. Confidence is our fuel. Our confidence, our belief that we can succeed, gets us started and helps us finish every challenge we tackle in life.

It is very important to understand the distinction between conditional and deeply rooted confidence. Conditional confidence balances precariously on shaky ground or may be just a façade. The healthy road to confidence is based on Christ. We all know people whose "confidence" is brash and overbearing, which is often a defense mechanism to mask insecurity. There are people whose confidence is based completely on their own merit and strength. This may be effective until they face rejection or until something they can't handle on their own comes along—and it always comes along.

If our confidence is based on other people or relationships, it is destined to crumble. I will never forget when my friend Kelly's world did just that.

Kelly's Story

When I discovered my husband of fourteen years was involved with my closest friend, many things were ripped from my life. I lost my husband and my best friend in one painful moment. The rejection felt like getting stabbed in the back by one person and in the chest by the other. I didn't know which way to fall. I was in the darkest hole of my life and felt there would never be a way out. I was alone with no one to trust.

My confidence was destroyed. Rejection says, "It's your fault." I was too fat or not talented enough. I wondered why anyone would ever want me.

I made many mistakes trying to fill the hole in my heart and refusing to wait on God's timing. I remarried, and my second husband cheated on me. I was desperate for someone to be with. If only I could have been confident being me.

Clinging to the fact that Jesus was also rejected began to change me (Isaiah 53:3). With His help, I chipped away at all the pain and anger. Healing took years—decades, really. I wouldn't give up. I told God, "I won't stop crying out to You for healing until I have it." The day I told my former best friend I forgave her, healing began to flow.

My confidence grew with every little miracle God did. When I was alone and it was just God and me, He worked in ways only He and I knew about. I learned I could trust Him. After years of pain and rejection, He has given me a wonderful

> man who truly loves me, but my confidence comes from something much deeper than our relationship. It doesn't come or go because I'm rejected, married, divorced, or single. I'm confident because of God's unshakable love for me. Never again will I allow anything created, such as a person or a situation, to take from me what the Creator Himself put in me.

From Where Do We Draw Our Confidence?

An infallible guarantee comes from only one place.

The well from which you draw your confidence makes all the difference. I discovered this in a very painful way. I mentioned before that I'm a naturally confident person. My mom says I came out that way. But I've learned that a confident personality based on self is not enough. My security wasn't built on solid ground. I still had to perform, succeed, look the part. I knew what the Bible said, and I truly believed it. But I was depending on my own strength to prop myself up. Because I drew my confidence from inside of myself, the rejection I experienced shook it so hard that it crumbled before my eyes.

Merriam-Webster defines *confidence* as "a feeling or consciousness of one's powers or of reliance on one's circumstances."[28] This describes where my confidence was, and that was my downfall. When my circumstances shifted beyond my control, I realized I had no power to change things. I thought this meant I was unworthy, and my confidence faltered. But that was wrong thinking.

I believe this Dictionary.com definition of *confidence* is much more accurate: "Full trust; belief in the powers, trustworthiness, or reliability of a person or thing…assurance."[29]

You can and should have belief in yourself—that's healthy—but "full trust" and "assurance," or an infallible guarantee, comes from only one place. This kind of confidence is found in Christ alone. I do believe in myself because God created me lovingly and with purpose, and I like who He made me to be. But I'm far from perfect. I cannot fully rely on my own power or my circumstances. However, I can be bold because of *His* power and faithfulness.

Proverbs 31 describes an "excellent woman" (v. 10 AMP). Verse 25 says, "She is clothed with strength and dignity; she can laugh at the days to come." This is a beautiful picture of confidence. The confident woman is a woman of strength and joy. When my confidence was based more on myself than it was founded in Christ, I had to constantly prove my worth. I had to make good grades, build a successful career, have a happy family... the list goes on. I didn't realize it at the time, but it was exhausting. I am now confident because of who God is, and I trust who He says I am. You can, too. You are loved, chosen, and called. Even when circumstances aren't what we want, when others hurt us, when we make mistakes, or when we aren't at our best, we can confidently stand on promises like the one in Proverbs 28:1, which says, "The righteous are as bold as a lion." It's your time to roar!

Claim Your Confidence

Now that you know how to draw your confidence from the right source, here are five helpful steps toward developing, or perhaps reclaiming, your confidence.

1. Act in a way that instills confidence.

Imagine what it would look like to act in confidence and then walk it out by practicing those actions. Be a person of integrity, kindness, and one who is

> *Be the kind of person you would entrust with your confidence.*

trustworthy. Be someone in whom you would be comfortable placing your confidence.

2. Begin doing things that build your confidence.

Think about what you view as confidence, and try some things in line with your vision. Begin small and work your way up. Master one, then try another. For example, first speak up in a conversation, then in a small group or meeting, and finally, if you're ready and want to, speak on stage in front of people. Choose a path that leads you to the goals you seek, and little by little you will prove to yourself that you can indeed succeed.

3. Redefine failure.

A setback does not define you. Don't generalize a failure and decide that it determines who you are. When failure happens, consider what you may learn from it, reexamine your goals and motives, adjust, go back to Scripture to fuel your confidence, and, at the right time, try again or attempt an appropriate variation. But whatever you do, don't allow the failure to try to destroy your growing confidence. Don't give up!

4. Avoid comparison.

When I learned about my husband's dependence on pornography, it crushed my confidence. He tried to assure me it wasn't about me, yet how could it not be? As my friend Mischelle said when she went through the same situation with her husband, "How can you win when you're fighting a fantasy?"

For the person who has faced a spouse who has cheated or has experienced a similar betrayal, comparisons are mountains to overcome. I sincerely feel your pain. But comparison is a death sentence to anyone's confidence. There will always be someone who is more successful, more intelligent, more attractive. Comparison is a trap leading you to feel less and less worthy, less capable, and less courageous until you are hopelessly lost. Instead, resist the temptation and remember that you can never look at someone else and see the entire picture of their life. We all have our blemishes and faults, but rarely do we share them.

When you learn to define your worth according to God's Word and not based on comparison to or the approval of others, you'll be free from this painful cycle of disappointment, and your deep need for acceptance and affirmation will be lovingly satisfied.

5. Embrace the truth of God's purpose for you.

God has put something beautiful in you. Confidence flows freely when you realize that you have a God-given purpose only you can accomplish. Give yourself the permission to love the you whom God created—the quirkiness, the flaws, the beauty. Remember:

> *Love the you whom God created.*

- Your beauty doesn't come from having someone say you're beautiful.
- Your talent doesn't only count when others recognize it.
- Your value exists even when others don't see or appreciate it.
- Your worth in Christ cannot be taken away.

There is always someone who needs your gifts, your kindness, your friendship, your wisdom, and your love. You are indispensable. The greatest confidence comes from embracing exactly who God created you to be.

Hold tightly to 2 Timothy 1:7: "For the Spirit God gave us does not make us timid, but gives us power, love and self-discipline."

Release the Pressure

As you walk through the steps toward healthy confidence, breathe a little and realize that you don't need to work up the confidence for the entire journey at once. Take it one day at a time. Confidence will grow with experience, success, and even failure, because you'll learn from that, too. Begin where you are, confident in the One who is walking each step with you and directing your path. Allow your confidence to blossom and grow from here.

To do this, we need what we read in the Bible. We need what God says about who we are and His love for us to move from words on a page to a heartfelt understanding deep in our souls. This is where confidence grows and healing takes place. Perhaps we must face some pain, even rejection, in life to learn not only to empathize with others' hurts, but to build confidence on a firm foundation—one that won't be shaken when our world is. I am better for having gone through the pain of rejection, despite the fact that Satan intended it to destroy me, to derail my purpose, and to leave me cowering. What he didn't expect is that in my weakness, I was made stronger (2 Corinthians 12:10).

Finally, as rejection attempts to hammer away at your confidence, rest assured that all is not lost. Refocus on the strength of Him who is your source. You can do this by spending focused time in prayer and reading Scriptures about how strong God is and how we can depend on Him to give us everything we need. Consider these:

> Do not be afraid; do not be discouraged. Go out to face them tomorrow, and the Lord will be with you.
>
> 2 Chronicles 20:17

> The Lord is my strength and my shield; my heart trusts in him, and he helps me. My heart leaps for joy, and with my song I praise him.
>
> Psalm 28:7

> Surely God is my salvation; I will trust and not be afraid. The Lord, the Lord himself, is my strength and my defense; he has become my salvation.
>
> Isaiah 12:2

> When I called, you answered me; you greatly emboldened me.
>
> Psalm 138:3

Isaiah 51 shouts the power of God and reminds us why our confidence in Him is secure:

> I, even I, am he who comforts you. Who are you that you fear mere mortals, human beings who are but grass, that you forget the Lord your Maker, who stretches out the heavens and who lays the foundations of the earth...For I am the Lord your God, who stirs up the sea so that its waves roar—the Lord Almighty is his name. I have put my words in your mouth and covered you with the shadow of my hand—I who set the heavens in place, who laid the foundations of the earth, and who say to Zion, "You are my people."
>
> Isaiah 51:12–13, 15–16

You are God's, and He is a *big* God. Confidence flourishes in an atmosphere of faith. When people do attack, try this: Be confident enough to let them be wrong about you. Stop defending yourself.

Let them believe what they will and keep moving forward, trusting that God's got your back, and know that He is your vindicator. You'll discover peace and power you didn't know before.

Nurture this seed of confidence. Replant it in the good soil of who Jesus declares you to be, and water it with His love and acceptance. Stretch yourself a bit. Place your full assurance in Him. Then just for fun, give yourself a high five and say, "You're pretty great, and your hair is fabulous!" This never hurts, either.

Lean in Closer

1. Rejection can "throw a bucket of cold water on the fires of confidence." How has feeling rejected caused you to lose confidence?
   _____
   _____

2. In what ways can you relate to Kelly's story?
   _____
   _____

3. What are some wells from which you have attempted to draw your confidence, and how did that work for you? Check the ones that apply and add others that may come to mind:
   - Talent
   - Intelligence
   - Appearance
   - Job
   - Money
   - Success
   - Gaining the acceptance of certain people
   - Family
   - Other:

Nurturing Confidence

_____
_____

4. Where does a lasting sense of real confidence come from? How can we access this lasting truth when our confidence feels shaky?
_____
_____

5. In what areas of your life would you like to be more confident?
_____
_____

6. Design your flight plan for healthy confidence, a runway from which it can soar:
   - What truths in God's Word about where your strength comes from will be your foundation? List a Bible verse or two that will encourage you.
     _____
     _____

   - What truths in God's Word about who God says you are will give you a lift? List a Bible verse or two that will propel you.
     _____
     _____

   - Based on God's Word, what truths about His promises for your purpose and future will fuel your confidence? List a verse or two that will sustain you.
     _____
     _____

CHAPTER 16

Developing Healthy Relationships

Joyce

Walk with the wise and become wise, for a companion of fools suffers harm.

Proverbs 13:20

Because of rejection and fear, I developed some detrimental relationship habits early in life, so I understand that learning to establish healthy relationships is important to the healing process. I am talking about connections that are mutually beneficial—not codependent, abusive, or destructive—but ones that draw you closer to your heavenly Father. I encourage you to begin praying for the right relationships.

The best practical advice I have for people when entering new relationships is to choose a person or a group of people who put God first in all they do. This doesn't necessarily mean a great relationship will develop, but it is a great foundation. In addition, it's important to choose people who are honest and trustworthy, who walk in integrity and have strong character, and who will be good, godly influences in your life. You'll also want someone you feel compatible with so the two of you will enjoy being together. These are general guidelines for a variety of relational scenarios.

Every Relationship Isn't Good for Every Person

As new people come into your life, be prayerful about the type of relationship you will have with them. I have heard that some people come into our lives for a reason, some come into our lives for a season, and some come to us for life. Some people will eventually become very close friends, and some will remain casual acquaintances. God knows what each relationship should be, and He will show us as we seek His guidance.

I think it is important to point out that not all people fit well together. Just because you want to be friends with someone doesn't mean the relationship would be good for you. If you feel rejected by someone you would like to be close to, it's possible that they may not be rejecting you; it may be that God is protecting you from something that would not be good for you if you were to become close to that person. Trusting God in all things protects us from much of the hurt we experience in life. We are commanded by God to love everyone (John 13:34). We can do this because God gives us the ability to love (Romans 5:5), but loving someone doesn't necessarily mean that a close friendship with that person will be a good fit.

I have known people who made it clear that they wanted to be close friends with me, but their personality and mine would not have been good together. This doesn't mean there is something wrong with them; it could mean that they are not a good fit for me or that I am not a good fit for them. I am friendly with them and appreciate them as individuals, but I don't need to try to be close friends with them just because that's the type of relationship they would like. If any of those people are insecure, they may feel rejected when I choose not to enter into a close friendship. But choosing not to invite them to do everything I do doesn't mean I am rejecting them. Each of us must find our security in Christ and not expect other people to make us feel good about ourselves.

Years ago, a woman who attended a weekly Bible study that I led told another attendee she felt I was rejecting her because I never took time to talk to her. I certainly didn't want to hurt her, but I honestly could not remember a single time when I ignored her. I didn't even remember seeing her very much. I prayed about this situation, and God showed me that He caused me not to see her because she was trying to get something from me that He wanted her to get from Him. She wanted to gain a sense of worth, value, and security from having my attention. Had I given it to her, she would have been disappointed because she was looking for something from me that she could get only from God.

> *Trying to be everyone's best friend is exhausting.*

Sometimes our values and interests are so different from another's that friendship would simply never work. Studies show we can only manage five close friends at one time,[30] and most people say they have between one and four good friends.[31] The person who tries to be everyone's best friend will be exhausted and is likely to end up with no true, deep, meaningful friendships.

Relationships and Personality Types

I think having insight into personality types can protect us from rejection. When we understand the basic personality types, we can better see why some people enjoy each other and do well in relationships together while others don't. If a relationship doesn't work out, we are able to see that our personality isn't a good match for someone else's, and vice versa, and we don't take the situation personally.

There are four basic personality types: sanguine, choleric, phlegmatic, and melancholy. Let's take a look at each one.

- *Sanguine:* Some personality types need people around them frequently, while others don't. The sanguine person, for example, wants and needs lots of interaction with people. Usually, a sanguine person would rather be with people than be alone. People who are sanguine are very social. They are enthusiastic and usually the life of the party. I know a woman married to a pastor who is sanguine, and he wants people with them all the time. She says, "People energize my husband, and they wear me out." This is a good example of how different people can be.
- *Choleric:* People who have a choleric personality type, as I do, may invest their time only in the people who help them

reach their goals. Of all the personality types, those who are choleric are more likely to hurt people's feelings and not even be aware they have done it. They tend to be dominating and focus more on results than feelings. They don't need a lot of close friends, and although they do want friends, they also enjoy having time alone. Learning to walk in love with all people has been invaluable to me. I can love someone and still not be in love with their personality.

- *Phlegmatic:* People with this personality type are easygoing and relaxed; they don't worry, and they don't focus on how others make them feel. Those who are phlegmatic probably wouldn't notice if they were being rejected, and if they did, they probably wouldn't care. Dave has a phlegmatic personality.
- *Melancholy:* People with a melancholy personality type are more likely than others to be hurt easily and perhaps even imagine rejection that is not real. Although they like privacy and prefer only a few close friends, they are sensitive to how people make them feel. By nature, they are not socially oriented. They are content to be alone, generally speaking, and they need a reason to be with others.

There is much more to learn about personality types, and it is fascinating. If you would like to know more, I recommend *Personality Plus* by Florence Littauer or *Spirit-Controlled Temperament* by Tim LaHaye. Both of these books helped me tremendously at a time in my life when I was struggling with many of my relationships. In addition, the Enneagram test and the Myers-Briggs Type Indicator are popular ways to gain insight into your personality and discover what strengths you can offer other people and what you need from them.

Most of us have a blend of more than one personality type.

Ginger is choleric/sanguine, so, as she puts it, she loves to have fun with many people around her and to tell others how to have fun, too. She is a leader who accomplishes a lot of good things.

As you can see, this general information about personality types doesn't provide a perfect fit for everyone, but it does give us an idea of how diverse we are. Each of the different personality types has strengths and weaknesses, and we should appreciate people's strengths and bear with their weaknesses (Romans 15:1).

Let me emphasize that God requires us to love everyone, but we don't have to spend a lot of time with someone we simply don't fit well with. Even Jesus seemed to have a closer relationship with Peter, James, and John than with the other disciples. Of these three, John appears to have had a more intimate relationship with Jesus than any of the disciples. Jesus didn't reject the others, but He knew what each of their futures would be and had a reason for spending more time with some than with others.

I have asked God to put in my life the people who are right for me. So, when a relationship doesn't seem to be working out, I just believe it must not be right for me. I don't even have to know why it isn't right. I simply trust God to protect me from any relationship that wouldn't be healthy or safe for me.

Motives

When we think of establishing healthy relationships, it's important to consider our motives. I've mentioned motives briefly in this book, but let's take a closer look at them here. What are your motives for the relationships you seek? Are they to be a blessing to other people—or to gain something from them? Or is your motive to find someone to meet your needs or somehow guarantee against rejection? Might your motive be to manipulate your way into something—an opportunity or an advantage—that perhaps you shouldn't have?

Developing Healthy Relationships

When I was younger and less experienced, I decided who I wanted to be friends with, and I often had the wrong motives. Maybe those people were part of the "popular" group, and I wanted to be in that group. Maybe I viewed them as important and thought I would be more important if they were my friends. When I did end up in those relationships, they always ended in a great deal of pain for me. Through these situations, God taught me to pray for divine relationships and not to choose people based on what they could do for me. Now I don't work at trying to force relationships with certain people; I pray and let them happen naturally if they are right for me.

If you expect too much in a relationship, you will drive people away from you and be disappointed. If you're out to please people more than to do what is right, you cannot sustain it long term. If you are looking to meet a need that only God can fill, other people will not meet it, and you will still feel empty even in relationship with them. And if you choose bad relationships because they are familiar or you don't feel you deserve better ones, they are destined to hurt you.

When I do have good relationships that are healthy for me, I work at maintaining them. Spending time with your friends will feed the relationship, and being available for them when they are hurting or have a need is very important. Everyone, it seems, is "busy" today, and due to this reality, we often let time with friends fall to the bottom of our list, if it is on the list at all. Anything will die if you don't feed it, including relationships.

There are many Bible verses that teach us to accept and love all people regardless of who they are, their situation, or background (Luke 10:25–37; Romans 2:11; Galatians 3:28). We won't become best friends with everyone, but God commissions us to love everyone, even our

> Love is not how you feel about a person but how you treat them.

enemies (Matthew 5:44). I'll say it again: Love is not how we feel about a person; it is how we treat them.

> Accept one another, then, just as Christ accepted you, in order to bring praise to God.
>
> Romans 15:7

We should accept and be kind to everyone, and we should try to make sure we don't cause anyone to feel rejected. But it is not our responsibility to make everyone feel good about themselves. Each person needs to find their security and value in Christ, not merely in how other people treat them.

Shaping or Correcting Others

In the early years of my marriage to Dave, I frequently expressed my unhappiness to him and told him what he needed to do to keep me happy. I was basically laying down laws that I expected him to follow—and that never works. God taught me not to give Dave the responsibility for my joy. It was my responsibility, not his.

> *Your joy is your responsibility.*

You won't find anyone who will always do what you want and never disappoint or hurt you. Dave is a wonderful husband. He is easygoing, and he lets me do what I want to do and go where I want to go. He rarely tells me no about anything. However, he is not a gift buyer, and giving and receiving gifts is one of my love languages—meaning one of the ways I express love and feel loved by others.

I also feel loved when people do acts of service to help me. Dave is great at acts of service. I have at times focused on the fact that he doesn't buy me gifts and told him how much I would like it if he did. Still, he doesn't do it. Of course, that hurts my feelings and makes me angry at times. Dave is a logical person, and he says, "I'll buy you anything you want and will take you to pick it out. But when I buy you things, you always take them back, so I might as well not waste my time."

Dave's logic is correct, but logic doesn't usually soothe someone's hurt feelings. I do often return things he gets me, but I want to know that he spent time at least trying to buy something for me. At the same time, I have learned that I can save myself a lot of misery by focusing on his good points, which far outnumber his bad ones!

I do want to report that, on my most recent birthday, Dave called the woman I buy most of my clothes from and told her to put together five entire outfits, including jewelry, and he went and picked them up. They were wrapped beautifully and were perfect because he got the right person to pick them out. This did make me very happy because he surprised me with these gifts. (He joked that since there were five gifts, they could count for five years.)

Most of us tend to focus on one or two things people do that we don't like, and we pay no attention to all the things they do that we do like. I would much rather Dave not buy me gifts and let me do what I want to than buy me gifts but not give me freedom to do things I desire to do.

I can't begin to remember all the times I tried to "correct" Dave about not buying me gifts. I defended myself and tried to change him, but it didn't work. I've decided to enjoy the man God has given me and stop trying to change him into someone else. The birthday surprise was nice, but I won't begin to expect it all the time. I'll enjoy what Dave does do and not feel rejected if he never gives me another gift. After all, he tells me he is my greatest gift!

Rejection and Communication

Communication is an essential part of relationships. Rejection puts a negative filter on the way we receive communication from others. For many years, Dave and I had a great difficulty communicating. We would start talking about something and end up arguing, and I couldn't understand how we got from where we started to the argument. Dave finally told me he felt the only way he could communicate with me was to agree with everything I said.

As I prayed about the situation, God showed me that if Dave didn't agree with my opinion, I felt he was rejecting me. I had to learn that just because someone rejected my *opinion*, it didn't mean they were rejecting *me*. We all need the freedom to share our opinion honestly when someone asks for it. Realizing this was a breakthrough for me, and it could be a breakthrough for you, too. We all have opinions, but they are not who we are; they are simply perspectives we have and usually give too freely. Parents of adult children need to be cautious in this area. Only give advice and opinions when asked. Or if you feel you must share, don't be offended or feel rejected if your advice or opinion is not received well.

The only way two people can enjoy a healthy relationship is to communicate honestly, and the only way they can do that is if they are both secure in who they are and who God has made them to be. Be secure enough to let people be honest with you. They could be wrong about what they are saying, but at least pray about it and then turn the matter over to God.

> *Be secure enough to let people be honest with you.*

The Blame Game

Humility is vital in relationships, and it is probably the most difficult virtue to develop and hold on to. When we've been hurt, it is easy to blame the people we are in relationship with for our pain. We are usually too proud to admit we could be at fault. Satan's sin was pride (Isaiah 14:12–14; Ezekiel 28:17), and he attacks all of us with pride. People who are rooted in rejection often use pride as a cover for the shame they feel. For example, for years, my fear of rejection kept me from asking for help. I did this because I knew I couldn't be rejected if I didn't ask anyone for anything. Instead, I always tried to do everything myself, so I didn't have to depend on anyone else—and that is pride.

Humility can talk about and admit its weaknesses, but pride must be strong in every area. If the prideful person isn't strong, they make excuses for it, deny it, or blame someone else for it. A healthy relationship cannot flourish in such an environment.

I am strong and have a lot of endurance. I believe God strengthened me as I endured abuse and other difficult situations, but nobody is strong in all areas, all the time. For a long time, it was important to me that I was never seen as weak. My mother was weak, and her weakness of character and inability to confront my father caused a lot of my pain. I hated weakness. But I learned to be vulnerable. It was scary, but I took steps of faith in that direction—baby steps at first. Now I talk about my weaknesses openly and ask for help often.

I'll also admit that I found weak people annoying. Those who whined about every little inconvenience and were afraid to try new things bothered me. But as I mentioned earlier in this chapter, God's Word tells us to bear with the failings of the weak (Romans 15:1). For everything we do incorrectly, God has a scripture that will help us change if we will let it work in our lives. Moving beyond being annoyed by people I viewed as weak took time, because first I had to be willing to change my attitude toward them—and realizing that I also had weaknesses helped me do that. The good news is that the Holy Spirit never gives up working with us and helping us become the person God created us to be. He never gave up on me, and He will never give up on you.

> The Holy Spirit never gives up.

Finding Balance

As with everything in life, balance is key in establishing healthy relationships. When you've been hurt, you may have learned to expect less of your relationships—or to demand more. You may push people away to avoid rejection, or you may hold them too tightly. None of these strategies work, but you do not have to remain stuck in patterns that continue to bring you more rejection. It may take time and a lot of prayer, but it is exciting to think that you can enjoy healthy, happy relationships. God can bring you divine connections and teach you new ways to interact with others. You are created to enjoy relationships that enrich your life and the lives of others.

Lean in Closer

1. What are some reasons you may not be able to develop close relationships with certain people?
   _____
   _____

2. Of the four personality types described in this chapter, which one is closest to your personality? How can understanding these personality types help you form good relationships?
   _____

3. Do you ever give other people responsibility for your happiness and joy? What positive steps can you take to move toward healthy relationships that benefit both you and the other person?

4. What is your biggest challenge in forming healthy relationships? Check all that apply and add others that come to mind:
    - I struggle to be honest.
    - I am defensive or argumentative.
    - I avoid anger or confrontation.
    - I choose unhealthy people or people who are not a good fit for me.
    - I expect too much from people.
    - I push people away.
    - Other:

5. What are your motives for the relationships you seek?

6. Pray now for God to bring you the people and relationships He wants for you.

CHAPTER 17

Five Choices That Bring Hope and Healing

Ginger

I have set before you life and death, blessings and curses. Now choose life, so that you and your children may live and that you may love the Lord your God, listen to his voice, and hold fast to him.

Deuteronomy 30:19–20

What happens now? Well, this is where things get real. This is a battle, and you must fight with everything you have within you and all that God gives you. Change comes with decision and determination. You have vital and powerful choices to make—choices with great potential to change your life or to leave you stuck in a cycle of pain.

You may also be facing exceptionally difficult decisions. Regarding a relationship you're in now, perhaps you're wondering:

- *Where do I go from here?*
- *Do I stay or go?*
- *Should I fight for this relationship?*
- *Is the other person willing to fight for this relationship also?*

I urge you: Ask the questions. Deal with the emotions. Don't shove them down or deny them. Get help if you need it; there is absolutely no shame in that. And offer everything to God, completely and honestly—the fear, disappointment, anger, confusion, all of it. Ask Him for comfort, direction, and healing as only He can give. If you're in this place, you are at a crossroads, and the choices you make are important steps toward the healing God wants to do in you.

Let's look at five important choices I believe will move you forward along your journey of healing, hope, and developing healthy relationships in the future:

1. Choose faith over feelings.
2. Choose to risk loving others.
3. Choose to forgive.

4. Choose to be grateful.
5. Choose to surrender.

Choose Faith Over Feelings

Continue to choose truth over lies and faith over feelings. Do explore your feelings and ask where they are coming from. Our feelings matter, but we cannot allow them to rule us. *Feeling* rejected is not always the same as *being* rejected. The choice is sometimes ours. We can choose to reject the rejection that is knocking at our door, to see it differently. At other times, rejection may as well be stamped on your paperwork: *Rejected*. No mistake; it is clear as day.

Even when we have been rejected, we still have a choice as to how we will respond. Feeling rejected should not mean *living* rejected. It's not the feeling that is the issue; it's what you choose to do with the feelings. Will you make a home in them, settle down with them, and see yourself through their lenses? Or will you deal with them and move on?

> *Feeling rejected should not mean living rejected.*

Do you ever get an annoying song stuck in your head? An excellent way to get rid of it is to replace it by thinking of a different song that you do like. In the same way, when rejection and pain and discouragement are stuck in your head, replace them with the truth of God's complete acceptance. Choose faith even when feelings say otherwise. And yes, God will help you. His Word says you can do it:

> Now what I am commanding you today is not too difficult for you or beyond your reach...No, the word is very near you; it is in your mouth and in your heart so you may obey it.
>
> Deuteronomy 30:11, 14

Continue to believe God's Word because that will build and strengthen your faith. When feelings of rejection come, remember Isaiah 49:16, which teaches that God engraves us on the palm of His hands. Choose to believe this truth instead of dwelling on the fact that you feel rejected. When you feel afraid, fight back with Isaiah 41:10, which says, "So do not fear, for I am with you; do not be dismayed, for I am your God. I will strengthen you and help you; I will uphold you with my righteous right hand." If feelings of hopelessness creep in, stir up your hope through Romans 15:13, which says, "May the God of hope fill you with all joy and peace as you trust in him, so that you may overflow with hope by the power of the Holy Spirit."

Choosing faith over feelings, trust over fear, and hope over hopelessness are not one-and-done decisions. You must choose over and over, day after day. Eventually, these choices begin to come more naturally. Before you know it, they are more than choices; they become a part of who you are. And God will always be with you through these battles.

Choose to Risk Loving Others

My dog, Winston, a scruffy little shichon who looks like a well-worn teddy bear, loves me. I mean, he *really* loves me. He wants little more than to snuggle up beside me, go for long walks together, and enjoy uninterrupted moments of direct eye contact. He follows me everywhere. I can barely go to the bathroom without him. I'm just trying to do what I need to do, and there he is with his big brown eyes looking up at me adoringly. He greets me with excitement every time I walk in the door, even if I only step out momentarily or, heaven forbid, thoughtlessly go to the mailbox without him. While there are times when I would take a little less devotion and a little more privacy, with Winston I am earnestly loved and have absolutely no risk of rejection.

Dogs are wonderful, but relationships with people are not meant to be like relationships with dogs; people are riskier than pups. We are flawed. We come with opinions, hurts, and needs. It isn't healthy to expect undivided attention, unwavering obedience, and overjoyed responses from our fellow human beings at every turn. We need love that is freely given and imperfect in its beauty. This means mistakes will be made, and we will at times feel the sting of rejection. But God made us for the joy and pain of relationships with imperfect people.

> God made us for the joy and pain of relationships with imperfect people.

The only way to be able to love others again after being hurt or rejected is to embrace risk. When you invest in a relationship, there are no guarantees. It doesn't matter if it's a friend, a family member, or a romantic interest, everyone has free will. Everyone has their own issues. Everyone fails—they do, I do, and so do you.

Some relationships are one-sided. Healthy relationships are not. Yes, there are seasons when we sow into people and receive little or nothing from them in return, when we invest in people out of love and not expectation. When the time comes and you know that the grace has lifted, it may be time for them to help themselves and for you to focus elsewhere. They may not like it when you change your approach to the relationship. They may treat you poorly and without gratitude. The rejection you experience in situations such as these hurts, but remember who you are and love them as you move on. Some people must be loved from a distance.

When it comes to relationships, not everyone will like you. Not everyone will like what you do. They may speak negatively and reject you, but without risk, our lives are static and without growth or joy. Loving others is risky; not loving is unbearable.

> Loving others is risky, but not loving is unbearable.

Choose to Forgive

We can't overemphasize the importance of forgiveness on your journey of healing from rejection. In fact, healing is impossible when you're nursing unforgiveness. It will keep the rejection stirred up and endlessly alive. Remember, we fight against the lies of rejection, not the person or the source of that rejection. The relationship involved may be restored, or it may be a lost cause—either way, we can forgive. Forgiveness is one of the best ways to reject the lies the enemy whispers to us and refuse to allow him to claim ground in our life.

> Therefore, as God's chosen people, holy and dearly loved, clothe yourselves with compassion, kindness, humility, gentleness and patience. Bear with each other and forgive one another if any of you has a grievance against someone. Forgive as the Lord forgave you. And over all these virtues put on love, which binds them all together in perfect unity.
> Colossians 3:12–14

> Don't say, "I'll pay you back for the evil you did." Wait for the Lord. He will make things right.
> Proverbs 20:22 ICB

You can't be bitter and be happy. Choosing to forgive will open the pathway to move forward full of the hope that Jesus longs to bring you. It will release you.

Choosing to forgive is often difficult, but it's necessary for experiencing freedom and healing. I know someone who knew she needed to forgive a friend for a deep hurt. She struggled to do it until one day, she found herself saying "Lord, I choose to forgive my friend, and I ask you to bless her" while driving past a road sign on her way to work. She decided that day to verbalize her forgiveness each day when she saw that sign while driving to work. The process took several weeks, but she was able to forgive her friend, and today their friendship is stronger than ever. Forgiveness did such a complete work that when asked what happened that caused my friend so much pain, she cannot even remember.

Choose to Be Grateful

I'm writing this on a perfect beach day. Tim and I are enjoying some time away, just the two of us. As I watch the waves gently roll in and out and enjoy the sea breeze caressing my face, I'm overwhelmed with gratitude.

We have spent hours together walking up and down the beach, soaking up the sunrises and enjoying the golden hours of sunset. In between, I can't help but notice how cute he looks in his floppy sun hat. He calls it his "doofus hat," which I think is hilarious and honestly appropriate. I'm also keenly aware that, had we both made different choices, we may not have had this sweet time.

As I look out on the calm waters, I remember the waves of shock and pain that tossed me relentlessly. I'm grateful Tim did what he needed to do to break free from all that held him, and that he fought for his freedom and chose Christ over everything else. I'm grateful God healed my broken heart and helped me forgive and trust again. Now I cling to that anchor of hope that is Christ, keeping me in place when the storms pick up and the waves threaten again.

> We have this hope as an anchor for the soul, firm and secure.
> Hebrews 6:19

> Then we will no longer be infants, tossed back and forth by the waves, and blown here and there.
> Ephesians 4:14

> God's promises are true.

As we mature in Christ, we learn how faithful God is. His promises are true, and I'm thankful for so many things He has done and taught me. When your life is overflowing with gratitude, there is less room for the lies of the enemy to find a place to perch. My heart is full. I am thankful for the life Tim and I have now—what we both fought for. I won't take a moment for granted.

> Give thanks for everything to God the Father in the name of our Lord Jesus Christ.
>
> Ephesians 5:20 NLT

Find and cling to what you are grateful for, whether it is a heart that is healing, new lessons learned, or hope for days ahead. Allow gratitude for what God has done to replace any regret, and be thankful for all God is doing to fill the void of rejection. Choose gratitude and share it with your Father. It truly changes your heart, even when times are tough—no, *especially* when times are tough. Tell Him:

- "Thank You for what You are doing in me, though I have far to go."
- "Thank You for this day even when the day isn't ideal."
- "Thank You for this moment, as imperfect as it may be."
- "Thank You for Your love, which will never reject me."

Choose to Surrender

I believe the most powerful choice we can make is complete surrender to God. So many of our other decisions and choices fall into place when we release everything into His hands. If you've never given your life to Him, begin there. Tell Him you need a Savior who will accept you completely. Ask for His forgiveness for your sins and confess Him as Lord of your life. Surrender your pain and your uncertainty.

Can you surrender to the God who is working on your behalf even when you don't see Him working yet or understand His ways? Even mature Christians who know the Word and love Jesus with all their heart still face disappointment. True surrender comes out of a decision to trust even then. He will not fail you.

Paul says in Ephesians 4:22–24 to put off your old self, to release old habits and defense mechanisms to reach for something better. He says we must surrender our attitudes and the way we once thought:

> You were taught, with regard to your former way of life, to put off your old self, which is being corrupted by its deceitful desires; to be made new in the attitude of your minds; and to put on the new self, created to be like God in true righteousness and holiness.

You are a beautiful new creation. When we surrender to a better way and choose to do as the Word says, we find blessing and freedom.

> But whoever looks intently into the perfect law that gives freedom, and continues in it—not forgetting what they have heard, but doing it—they will be blessed in what they do.
>
> James 1:25

It is time to turn everything over to God. Consider offering Him this prayer from your heart right now:

Lord, I surrender my life to You, along with any lies I've held on to. I give You the rejection I am dealing with to use for Your glory and my good. Please take the things I've held on to in anger and unforgiveness. Forgive me, and help me to forgive others. I give You my insecurity and my wounds and ask that You heal them. I surrender my pride and give up the way I thought my life would be, in exchange for something better in Your hands. I love You and choose today to give You everything.

With all my heart, I encourage you to surrender your rejection, your pain, your pride, your life to Jesus. You will not be sorry you did.

Give Yourself Time

If the rejection you're currently dealing with has happened recently, give yourself time to move beyond the shock of it. Today may not be the day for life-changing decisions, but it can be a day of one small healthy choice, such as one of the choices mentioned in this chapter. Even if the rejection wound is fresh, you can still choose faith over feelings or you can still choose to surrender. You get to choose which choice or choices you make right now, and I encourage you to take just one small step toward health and healing.

To those who have experienced what I have, or who have perhaps known the pain of someone hurting you in a similar way: If you have faced abuse or endured an unhealthy relationship, the many decisions to be made may overwhelm your mind. Don't attempt to tackle all of them at once. Answers become clearer as you face them one by one. Allow yourself grace. You're going through an incredibly difficult time.

When I discovered what Tim had been doing, I remember being so hurt and asking God what choice I should make—to stay with my husband or to leave him. Staying was risky; it was hard. In situations like these, all options are difficult. There are no 100 percent guarantees. For Tim and me, there were important considerations to make, such as defining ground rules, putting media filters in place, establishing accountability, and navigating many long, difficult conversations.

Our journey was far from perfect. The road through a situation like this is fraught with peril, U-turns, and detours. Tim and I were both committed and fought hard, but I am well aware it doesn't always work for everyone as it has worked for us. I know many people whose spouses did not make the hard choices, whose relationships did not survive. In fact, one of my friends who went through a similar situation with her husband and who helped me through my terrible time eventually lost her marriage. But today, she and many others I know are healed and whole. With time and God's help, they are happier than they ever thought they could be. If you find yourself walking this road without your spouse, you will not be alone! God will never, *never* reject you.

Who Do You Choose to Be?

I remember struggling with the decision to stay in my marriage because it felt weak to do so. I thought, *I don't want to be that woman who puts up with this stuff.* But it doesn't matter what anyone else thought; only I could choose what I would do and who I would be. I wasn't putting up with anything; I was choosing to fight for our marriage—for it to be healed and to become more of what God intended to begin with, for me to love and be loved as Christ loves the church (Ephesians 5:25). I wasn't asking for perfection, but neither would I settle. What I chose took courage and strength. Whether our relationship survived or not, I chose to stand on who God says I am, no matter how rejected I felt, because in Him I was wanted and adored.

When it comes to who you will be, what choices will you make? Whatever heartbreak or type of rejection you face, God's promises are true. First Corinthians 1:9 assures us, "God is faithful (reliable, trustworthy, and therefore ever true to His promise, and He can be depended on); by Him you were called into companionship and participation with His Son, Jesus Christ our Lord" (AMPC). But remember, you must choose to walk in God's promises. Don't allow that little word *but* to sabotage you.

- "I know what God's Word says, *but*..."
- "I could be over this, *but*..."
- "I would forgive them, *but*..."
- "I would be happy, *but*..."

Instead say, *"But God!"* With His help, you can overcome all the negative, questioning thoughts. With Him, you can say, "I am a child of the King." You can proclaim, "I am whole in Christ—with or without the acceptance of others, with or without this relationship. I have His peace. I am forgiven. I am confident because of who He says I am." Know God's promises and choose to stand firm.

Lean in Closer

1. Where are you in your healing process in your fight against rejection? Where would you like to be?

_____

_____

Five Choices That Bring Hope and Healing

2. Listed below are the issues we need to deal with when overcoming rejection. Select one or two to work on, and ask the Lord to help you:
   - Choose faith over feelings
   _____
   _____

   - Believe who God says I am
   _____
   _____

   - Trust God in order to embrace risk
   _____
   _____

   - Choose to forgive
   _____
   _____

   - Choose to be grateful
   _____
   _____

   - Choose to surrender to God
   _____
   _____

3. Read Ephesians 4:22–24. What parts of your old self do you need to put aside? What steps can you take to put on the new self?
   _____
   _____

4. How do verses like Deuteronomy 30:11, 14 and 1 Corinthians 1:9 encourage you to believe God will help you to make the right choices in dealing with rejection?
   _____
   _____

5. Write down a few additional Scripture verses that will help you live out your commitments. You may find them within the pages of this book, on the internet, or in a concordance. Keep these verses in front of you and even read them aloud to encourage your faith.

   _____

   _____

6. Are you ready to surrender your rejection, your pain, your pride, and your life to Jesus?

   _____

   _____

CONCLUSION

Joyce and Ginger

I have loved you with an everlasting love; I have drawn you with unfailing kindness.

Jeremiah 31:3

What should your healing from rejection look like? When Jesus healed people in the Bible, it did not always look the same for each one. Some He prayed for, others He touched, and some He instructed to go do something. Your experience won't be exactly like anyone else's; your healing is a gift designed for you. First Peter 5:10 says that God Himself will "restore you and make you strong, firm and steadfast." God will give you everything you need.

You may be asking yourself:

- *Can I really be healed?*
- *Can I count on what Scripture says?*
- *Is God truly faithful?*
- *Is the fact that He won't reject me enough to carry me through?*

These are honest questions, and it's okay to ask them. Many answers will come from time and experience with God. He is the only one who can heal our wounds. God has proven faithful in our lives and in countless others. His love *is* big enough to heal you.

What we have dealt with in this book is not easy stuff. We have lived the pain that comes with rejection, so we are not thoughtlessly suggesting scriptures to appease you. The Word of God is powerful, but when people are bleeding, coldly repeating Bible verses is not the answer. They need compassion, love, and time for the Holy Spirit to work. Jesus is so much more than "religion" and going through the motions. He is love embodied and given for us; He sacrificed everything so we can live in victory beyond any rejection or heartbreak.

Healing does takes time, so please be patient with yourself and enjoy every little victory you win. Allow yourself to experience the grace and mercy that God extends to you. Don't ever give up. Study God's Word and trust that He is not finished with you yet. The road out of rejection can be long, but it is the road to true joy and peace that surpasses understanding. There are intersections to cross and choices to be made. As we begin to see God's faithfulness, the promises in the Bible become real and experiential. They are life!

If you could ask people throughout time if God's love and acceptance is big enough to cover rejection, countless individuals would shout "Undoubtedly, yes!" Even though God's acceptance is a well-established truth for generations of people who have experienced it, each of us must answer these questions for ourselves:

- *Will I allow God's truth to be true in my life?*
- *Will I open the door for God's acceptance to do its work—to be more powerful than the rejection I'm feeling?*
- *Will I allow the truth of God's acceptance to grow deep roots and bountiful fruit in my soul?*

Your story is not over. Rejection is a chapter—yes, a painful one—but there's much more to be written. There are times when we *feel* loved and accepted—and everything seems warm, cozy, and wonderful. There are also times we don't feel loved or accepted, and those can be cold and harsh. When difficult experiences and feelings come, we face them and refocus on what we know is true. We remember that we are unconditionally loved and accepted—and there's not a moment when we are not.

We can't promise you will never experience rejection again, but we can promise you that it will never be from God. Yes, our lives are shaped by our experiences, by our decisions, and by the things other people do. Rejection from people who should have loved us better or those who should have had no authority in our lives at all has an impact on us, sometimes in significant ways. But they do not get the final word, and the enemy does not get the final say. Their influence will fade as we are beautifully molded by the loving hands of Jesus. God is working. He will heal you and give you favor with the right people. A new day is dawning. Good things are on their way to you right now. Be expecting them at any moment. God is lovingly working in you and with you. He is carefully handwriting the story of your life, and it is one of healing, faith, and confidence—a tale of renewed trust, strength, and victory.

FIGHTING FOR THE REJECTED

Joyce and Ginger

If you pour yourself out for the hungry and satisfy the desire of the afflicted, then shall your light rise in the darkness and your gloom be as the noonday.

Isaiah 58:10 ESV

Healing often comes when we reach out to help someone. Proverbs 31:8–9 tells us, "Speak up for those who cannot speak for themselves, for the rights of all who are destitute. Speak up and judge fairly; defend the rights of the poor and needy."

We have had the privilege and heartbreak of traveling the world and witnessing firsthand the plight of far too many women and girls. The rejection they face worldwide is abhorrent. Many are completely discounted as people, unseen and ignored, treated as less than cattle or other property. Others are told outright that they are worthless. They are used and abused. They are sold to provide income for their families. In some places, baby girls are killed simply because they are seen as having no value. We've seen what human trafficking and other such horrendous injustices—such as denying girls education and forcing them into child marriages—do to women, as well as the price that is paid by their families, communities, and entire cultures.

Because of the abuse I (Joyce) faced, my heart is particularly burdened to help others who have suffered in the ways I did.

Project GRL was birthed out of that passion for women everywhere to experience the healing I've experienced and to help meet their physical needs. Through education programs, fresh-water initiatives, anti–human trafficking efforts, sharing the truth of God's Word, and instilling value, we are seeing the lives of women and girls change every single day.

One of the best ways to honor God and get the devil back for the damage he has done is to reach out with the love of Jesus to as many people as we can. God says through the prophet Isaiah:

> Is not this the kind of fasting I have chosen: to loose the chains of injustice and untie the cords of the yoke, to set the oppressed free and break every yoke? Is it not to share your food with the hungry and to provide the poor wanderer with shelter—when you see the naked, to clothe them, and not to turn away from your own flesh and blood? Then your light will break forth like the dawn, and your healing will quickly appear; then your righteousness will go before you, and the glory of the Lord will be your rear guard. Then you will call, and the Lord will answer; you will cry for help, and he will say: Here am I.
>
> Isaiah 58:6–9

You can fight for the rejected around the world and in the United States through Project GRL. Helping others who have experienced what you have experienced is one way you can overcome evil with good, and it aids in your own healing.

Together, we can accomplish far more than any of us can on our own. It's time for girls everywhere to know they are extremely valuable and for your gloom to be bright as the noonday. You can make a difference. Please visit ProjectGRL.org to help today.

Do you have a real relationship with Jesus?

God loves you! He created you to be a special, unique, one-of-a-kind individual, and He has a specific purpose and plan for your life. And through a personal relationship with your Creator—God—you can discover a way of life that will truly satisfy your soul.

No matter who you are, what you've done, or where you are in your life right now, God's love and grace are greater than your sin—your mistakes. Jesus willingly gave His life so you can receive forgiveness from God and have new life in Him. He's just waiting for you to invite Him to be your Savior and Lord.

If you are ready to commit your life to Jesus and follow Him, all you have to do is ask Him to forgive your sins and give you a fresh start in the life you are meant to live. Begin by praying this prayer...

Lord Jesus, thank You for giving Your life for me and forgiving me of my sins so I can have a personal relationship with You. I am sincerely sorry for the mistakes I've made, and I know I need You to help me live right.

Your Word says in Romans 10:9, "If you declare with your mouth, 'Jesus is Lord,' and believe in your heart that God raised him from the dead, you will be saved" (NIV). I believe You are the Son of God and confess You as my Savior and Lord. Take me just as I am, and work in my heart, making me the person You want me to be. I want to live for You, Jesus, and I am so grateful that You are giving me a fresh start in my new life with You today.

I love You, Jesus!

It's so amazing to know that God loves us so much! He wants to have a deep, intimate relationship with us that grows every day as we spend time with Him in prayer and Bible study. And we want to encourage you in your new life in Christ.

Please visit joycemeyer.org/KnowJesus to request Joyce's book *A New Way of Living*, which is our gift to you. We also have other free resources online to help you make progress in pursuing everything God has for you.

Congratulations on your fresh start in your life in Christ! We hope to hear from you soon.

SOURCE NOTES

Unless otherwise noted, Scripture quotations are taken from the Holy Bible, New International Version®, NIV®. Copyright ©1973, 1978, 1984, 2011 by Biblica, Inc.™ Used by permission of Zondervan. All rights reserved worldwide. www.zondervan.com. The "NIV" and "New International Version" are trademarks registered in the United States Patent and Trademark Office by Biblica, Inc.™

Scripture quotations marked AMPC are taken from the Amplified® Bible. Copyright © 1954, 1958, 1962, 1964, 1965, 1987 by The Lockman Foundation. Used by permission. www.Lockman.org.

Scripture quotations marked CEV are from the Contemporary English Version. Copyright © 1991, 1992, 1995 by American Bible Society. Used by permission.

Scripture quotations marked ESV are taken from The Holy Bible, English Standard Version. ESV® Text Edition: 2016. Copyright © 2001 by Crossway Bibles, a publishing ministry of Good News Publishers.

Scripture quotations marked MSG are taken from THE MESSAGE, copyright © 1993, 1994, 1995, 1996, 2000, 2001, 2002 by Eugene H. Peterson. Used by permission of NavPress. All rights reserved. Represented by Tyndale House Publishers, Inc.

Scripture quotations marked NKJV are taken from the New King James Version®. Copyright © 1982 by Thomas Nelson. Used by permission. All rights reserved.

Scripture quotations marked NLT are taken from the Holy Bible, New Living Translation, copyright ©1996, 2004, 2007, 2013, 2015 by Tyndale House Foundation. Used by permission of Tyndale House Publishers, Inc., Carol Stream, Illinois 60188. All rights reserved.

Scripture quotations marked AMP are from the Amplified® Bible. Copyright © 2015 by The Lockman Foundation. Used by permission. www.lockman.org.

All Scripture marked with the designation GW is taken from GOD'S WORD®. © 1995, 2003, 2013, 2014, 2019, 2020 by God's Word to the Nations Mission Society. Used by permission.

Scripture quotations marked KJV are taken from the King James Version of the Bible.

Scripture quotations marked TPT are from The Passion Translation®. Copyright © 2017, 2018, 2020 by Passion & Fire Ministries, Inc. Used by permission. All rights reserved. ThePassionTranslation.com.

Scripture quotations marked ICB are taken from The Holy Bible, International Children's Bible® Copyright© 1986, 1988, 1999, 2015 by Thomas Nelson. Used by permission.

1. "Children and Teens: Statistics," RAINN, https://rainn.org/statistics/children-and-teens.
2. "Youth Homelessness Overview," National Conference of State Legislatures, https://www.ncsl.org/human-services/youth-homelessness-overview.
3. "Reject," *American Heritage Dictionary of the English Language*, 5th ed. (Houghton Mifflin Harcourt, 2016).
4. "Reject," *Random House Webster's College Dictionary* (Random House, 2020).
5. "Reject," *Collins English Dictionary—Complete and Unabridged*, 12th ed. (HarperCollins, 2014).
6. "Reject," Merriam-Webster.com, https://www.merriam-webster.com/dictionary/reject.
7. "Delight," Merriam-Webster.com, https://www.merriam-webster.com/dictionary/delight.
8. Kirsten Weir, "The Pain of Social Rejection," *Monitor on Psychology*, 43, no. 4 (2012): 50, https://www.apa.org/monitor/2012/04/rejection.

Source Notes

9. Elitsa Dermendzhiyska, "Rejection Kills," Aeon, April 30, 2019, https://aeon.co/essays/health-warning-social-rejection-doesnt-only-hurt-it-kills.

10. George M. Slavich, Baldwin M. Way, Naomi I. Eisenberger, and Shelley E. Taylor, "Neural Sensitivity to Social Rejection Is Associated with Inflammatory Responses to Social Stress," *Proceedings of the National Academy of Sciences* 107, no. 33 (2010): 14817–14822, www.ncbi.nlm.nih.gov/pmc/articles/PMC2930449.

11. Weir, "The Pain of Social Rejection."

12. Eric Hickey, *Serial Murderers and Their Victims* (Wadsworth, 1997).

13. "Shame," APA Dictionary of Psychology, https://dictionary.apa.org/shame.

14. Henry Cloud, *Trust: Knowing When to Give It, When to Withhold It, How to Earn It, and How to Fix It When It Gets Broken* (Worthy, 2023), 90.

15. Beau Laviolette, "The 25% Rule: You Can't Please Everybody," Therapy Teacher.com, August 5, 2019, https://www.therapyteacher.com/blog/the-25-rule-you-can-t-please-everyone.

16. Sun Tzu, *The Art of War* (Sweet Water Press, 2006).

17. "How Your Heart Works," British Heart Foundation, https://www.bhf.org.uk/informationsupport/how-a-healthy-heart-works.

18. "How Your Body Replaces Blood," NHS Blood and Transplant, https://www.blood.co.uk/the-donation-process/after-your-donation/how-your-body-replaces-blood.

19. Mark Fischetti and Jen Christiansen, "Our Bodies Replace Billions of Cells Every Day," *Scientific American*, April 1, 2021, https://www.scientificamerican.com/article/our-bodies-replace-billions-of-cells-every-day.

20. "Amazing Heart Facts," *Nova*, https://www.pbs.org/wgbh/nova/heart/heartfacts.html.

21. "Lincoln's 'Failures'?" Abraham Lincoln Online, https://www.abrahamlincolnonline.org/lincoln/education/failures.htm.

22. "If You Believe in Yourself...," MotivateUs.com, https://motivateus.com/stories/famous-failures.htm.

23. "An Acting Class Refused a Sixteen-year-old Lucille Ball and Said That She Had 'No Talent,'" MeTV, September 17, 2024, https://www.metv.com/stories/an-acting-class-refused-a-sixteen-year-old-lucille-ball-and-said-that-she-had-no-talent.

24. "Poetry," Emily Dickinson Museum, https://www.emilydickinsonmuseum.org/emily-dickinson/poetry.

25. "Harrison Ford Was Told He'd Never Be a Star," News24.com, December 1, 2023, https://www.news24.com/you/archive/harrison-ford-was-told-hed-never-be-a-star-20170728-2.

26. "Walt Disney Quotes," BrainyQuote, https://www.brainyquote.com/quotes/walt_disney_130929.

27. Virgie Townsend, "Breaking the Abuse Cycle," *New York Times*, April 15, 2019, https://www.nytimes.com/2019/04/15/well/family/breaking-the-abuse-cycle.html.

28. "Confidence," Merriam-Webster.com, https://www.merriam-webster.com/dictionary/confidence.

29. "Confident," Dictionary.com, https://www.dictionary.com/browse/confidence.

30. Lindsay Holmes, "Science Says You Can Really Only Have 5 Close Friends at a Time," *HuffPost*, May 4, 2016, https://www.huffpost.com/entry/dunbar-layers-friendship-study_n_5728d4c5e4b016f37893ac14.

31. Isabel Goddard, "What Does Friendship Look Like in America?" Pew Research Center, October 12, 2023, https://www.pewresearch.org/short-reads/2023/10/12/what-does-friendship-look-like-in-america.

Joyce Meyer is one of the world's leading practical Bible teachers and a *New York Times* bestselling author. Joyce's books have helped millions of people find hope and restoration through Jesus Christ. Joyce's program, *Enjoying Everyday Life*, is broadcast to millions worldwide in 113 languages.

Through Joyce Meyer Ministries, Joyce teaches internationally on a number of topics with a particular focus on how the Word of God applies to our everyday lives. Her candid communication style allows her to share openly and practically about her experiences so others can apply what she has learned to their lives.

Joyce has authored more than 150 books, which have been translated into more than 164 combined languages, and over 42.5 million of her books have been distributed worldwide. Bestsellers include *Power Thoughts*; *The Confident Woman*; *Look Great, Feel Great*; *Starting Your Day Right*; *Ending Your Day Right*; *Approval Addiction*; *How to Hear from God*; *Beauty for Ashes*; and *Battlefield of the Mind*.

Joyce's passion to help people who are hurting is foundational to the vision of Hand of Hope, the missions arm of Joyce Meyer Ministries. Each year Hand of Hope provides millions of meals for the hungry and malnourished, installs freshwater wells in poor and remote areas, provides critical relief after natural disasters, and offers free medical and dental care to thousands through their hospitals and clinics worldwide. Through Project GRL, women and children are rescued from human trafficking and provided safe places to receive an education, nutritious meals, and the love of God.

Ginger Stache is an Emmy Award–winning television producer, author, and the chief creative officer of Joyce Meyer Ministries, leading the ministry's media areas, including broadcast and print. With a passion to elevate creativity, share God's love, and inspire others to help the forgotten, Ginger will take every opportunity to encourage people to step out of their routines and embrace the awe and wonder God has for them in all things and the joy in each day.

A firm believer in the power of compassion and relentlessly fighting for justice, she has traveled the world sharing stories of extraordinary individuals who have triumphed over immense challenges and encouraging others that they can do the same. She is especially passionate about empowering women and girls through the ministry's Project GRL initiatives, inspiring them to recognize their value and the impact they can have in the world.

Ginger can be seen on Joyce's *Enjoying Everyday Life* program and hosting *Joyce Meyer's Talk It Out* podcast. She is a wife, mother, and Gigi, roles that she holds dear. She and her husband, Tim, live in Missouri with their scruffy pup, Winston. You can connect with her on Instagram and Facebook @gingerlstache.

JOYCE MEYER MINISTRIES

U.S. & FOREIGN OFFICE ADDRESSES

Joyce Meyer Ministries
P.O. Box 655
Fenton, MO 63026
USA
(636) 349-0303

Joyce Meyer Ministries—Canada
P.O. Box 7700
Vancouver, BC V6B 4E2
Canada
(800) 868-1002

Joyce Meyer Ministries—Australia
Locked Bag 77
Mansfield Delivery Centre
Queensland 4122
Australia
(07) 3349 1200

Joyce Meyer Ministries—England
P.O. Box 8267
Reading RG6 9TX
United Kingdom
01753 831102

Joyce Meyer Ministries—South Africa
Unit EB06, East Block
Tannery Park, 23 Belmont Road
Rondebosch, Cape Town
South Africa 7700
(27) 21-701-1056

Joyce Meyer Ministries—Francophonie
BP 53, 77832 Ozoir la Ferriere
France
+33 610 288 944

Joyce Meyer Ministries—Germany
Bachstr. 1
22083 Hamburg
Germany
+49 (0)40 / 88 88 4 11 11

Joyce Meyer Ministries—Netherlands
P.O. Box 55, 7000 AB
Doetinchem
The Netherlands
+31 657 555 9789

Joyce Meyer Ministries—Russia
P.O. Box 789
Moscow 101000
Russia
+7 (985) 233-56-30

OTHER BOOKS BY JOYCE MEYER

100 Inspirational Quotes
100 Ways to Simplify Your Life
21 Ways to Finding Peace and Happiness
The Answer to Anxiety
Any Minute
Approval Addiction
The Approval Fix
*Authentically, Uniquely You**
The Battle Belongs to the Lord
*Battlefield of the Mind**
Battlefield of the Mind Bible
Battlefield of the Mind for Kids
Battlefield of the Mind for Teens
Battlefield of the Mind Devotional
Battlefield of the Mind New Testament
*Be Anxious for Nothing**
Be Joyful
Beauty for Ashes
Beginning Your Day God's Way
Being the Person God Made You to Be
*Blessed in the Mess**
Change Your Words, Change Your Life
Colossians: A Biblical Study
The Confident Mom
The Confident Woman
The Confident Woman Devotional
The Courage to Change
*Do It Afraid**
Do Yourself a Favor...Forgive
Eat the Cookie...Buy the Shoes
Eight Ways to Keep the Devil under Your Feet
Ending Your Day Right
Enjoying Where You Are on the Way to Where You Are Going
Ephesians: A Biblical Study
The Everyday Life Bible
The Everyday Life Psalms and Proverbs
Filled with the Spirit
Finding God's Will for Your Life
Galatians: A Biblical Study
Good Health, Good Life
Habits of a Godly Woman
*Healing the Soul of a Woman**

Healing the Soul of a Woman Devotional
Healing the Wounds of Rejection
Hearing from God Each Morning
How to Age without Getting Old
*How to Hear from God**
How to Succeed at Being Yourself
How to Talk with God
I Dare You
*If Not for the Grace of God**
In Pursuit of Peace
In Search of Wisdom
James: A Biblical Study
The Joy of an Uncluttered Life
The Joy of Believing Prayer
The Keys to a Happy and Healthy Marriage
Knowing God Intimately
A Leader in the Making
Life in the Word
Living beyond Your Feelings
Living Courageously
Look Great, Feel Great
Love Out Loud
The Love Revolution
Loving People Who Are Hard to Love
Making Good Habits, Breaking Bad Habits
Making Marriage Work (previously published as *Help Me—I'm Married!*)
Managing Your Emotions
*Me and My Big Mouth!**
*The Mind Connection**
Mornings with God
My Time with God
Never Give Up!
Never Lose Heart
New Day, New You
Overcoming Every Problem
Overload
The Pathway to Success
The Penny
Perfect Love (previously published as *God Is Not Mad at You*)*
Philippians: A Biblical Study
The Power of Being Positive
The Power of Being Thankful
The Power of Determination
The Power of Forgiveness
The Power of Simple Prayer

Power Thoughts
Power Thoughts Devotional
Powerful Thinking
Quiet Times with God Devotional
Reduce Me to Love
The Secret Power of Speaking God's Word
The Secrets of Spiritual Power
The Secret to True Happiness
Seven Things That Steal Your Joy
Start Your New Life Today
Starting Your Day Right
Straight Talk
Teenagers Are People Too!
Trusting God Day by Day
Uniquely You
*What About Me?**
The Word, the Name, the Blood
Woman to Woman
You Can Begin Again
*Your Battles Belong to the Lord**

JOYCE MEYER SPANISH TITLES

Amar a la gente que es difícil de amar (Loving People Who Are Hard to Love)
Auténtica y única (Authentically, Uniquely You)
Belleza en lugar de cenizas (Beauty for Ashes)
Benedicion en el desorden (Blessed in the Mess)
Buena salud, buena vida (Good Health, Good Life)
Cambia tus palabras, cambia tu vida (Change Your Words, Change Your Life)
El campo de batalla de la mente (Battlefield of the Mind)
Cómo envejecer sin avejentarse (How to Age without Getting Old)
Como formar buenos habitos y romper malos habitos (Making Good Habits, Breaking Bad Habits)
La conexión de la mente (The Mind Connection)
Dios no está enojado contigo (God Is Not Mad at You)
La dosis de aprobación (The Approval Fix)
Efesios: Comentario biblico (Ephesians: Biblical Commentary)
Empezando tu día bien (Starting Your Day Right)
Hágalo con miedo (Do It Afraid)
Hazte un favor a ti mismo…perdona (Do Yourself a Favor…Forgive)
Madre segura de sí misma (The Confident Mom)
Momentos de quietud con Dios (Quiet Times with God Devotional)
Mujer segura de sí misma (The Confident Woman)
No se afane por nada (Be Anxious for Nothing)
Pensamientos de poder (Power Thoughts)

Sanidad para el alma de una mujer (Healing the Soul of a Woman)
Sanidad para el alma de una mujer, devocionario (Healing the Soul of a Woman Devotional)
Santiago: Comentario bíblico (James: Biblical Commentary)
Sobrecarga (Overload)*
Sus batallas son del Señor (Your Battles Belong to the Lord)
Termina bien tu día (Ending Your Day Right)
Tienes que atreverte (I Dare You)
Usted puede comenzar de nuevo (You Can Begin Again)
Viva amando su vida (Living a Life You Love)
Viva valientemente (Living Courageously)
Vive por encima de tus sentimientos (Living beyond Your Feelings)
Y que hay de mi (What About Me?)

* Study Guide available for this title

Books by Dave Meyer

Life Lines